TYPE 2 DIABETES COOKBOOK FOR BEGINNERS

1500 Days of Easy & Tasty Recipes for the Newly Diagnosed with a 28-Day Meal Plan to Managing Prediabetes & Type 2 Diabetes without Sacrificing Taste

WRITTEN BY:

LISA SHERMAN

Table of Contents

Introduction

Diabetes is a disease in which blood glucose, also called blood sugar, doesn't get properly regulated. Glucose is the form of sugar that's used by all cells for energy. In diabetes, the body either doesn't produce enough insulin or can't use the insulin that's produced. This a type of disease that occurs when the pancreas can't produce enough insulin, a hormone that is used to help cells use glucose (sugar) for energy. Diabetics must monitor their glucose levels regularly and take insulin to make sure the glucose stays within the normal range.

Diabetes symptoms include excessive thirst, frequent urination, hunger, blurred vision, unexplained weight loss, and sudden numbness or weakness of the arms or legs. Diabetics also experienced excessive sweating, itching, and a dry mouth.

Diabetes is also a disease associated with blood sugar i.e., the concentration of sugar in the blood that the body is unable to maintain within normal limits.

Hyperglycemia occurs when blood glucose exceeds 100 mg./dl fastings or 140 mg/dl two hours after a meal. This condition may depend on a defect in function or a deficit in the production of insulin, the hormone secreted by the pancreas, used for the metabolism of sugars and other components of food to be transformed into energy for the whole organism (such as petrol for the engine).

When blood glucose levels are twice equal to or greater than 126 mg./dl, diabetes is diagnosed. High blood glucose levels—if not treated—over time, lead to chronic complications with damage to the kidneys, retina, nerves peripheral, and cardiovascular system (heart and arteries).

Causes of Diabetes and Risk Factors

Although some of the causes are completely unclear, even trivial viral infections are recognized, which can affect insulin-producing cells in the pancreas, such as:

- Measles.
- Cytomegalovirus.
- Epstein-Barr.
- Coxsackievirus.

For type 2 diabetes, however, the main risk factors are:

- Overweight and obesity.
- Genetic factors: family history increases the risk of developing type 2 diabetes.
- Ethnicity: the highest number of cases is recorded in the populations of sub-Saharan Africa and the Middle East and North Africa.
- Environmental factors are especially related to incorrect lifestyles (sedentary lifestyle and obesity).
- Gestational diabetes, which is diabetes that happens during pregnancy.
- Age: type 2 diabetes increases with increasing age, especially above the age of 65.
- Diet high in fat promotes obesity.
- Alcohol consumption.

- Sedentary lifestyle.

Signs and Symptoms of Diabetes

Symptoms of the disease, which depend on blood sugar levels, are:

- Polyuria, i.e., the high amount of urine production even during the night (nocturia).
- Polydipsia (an intense feeling of thirst).
- Polyphagia (intense hunger).
- Dry mucous membranes (the body's need to replenish fluids and severe dehydration).
- Asthenia (feeling tired).
- Weight loss.
- Frequent infections.
- Blurred vision.

In type 1 diabetes they manifest rapidly and with great intensity. In type 2 diabetes, on the other hand, symptoms are less evident, develop much slower, and may go unnoticed for months or years. Diagnosis often occurs by chance, on the occasion of tests done for any reason: the finding of a glycemia greater than 126 mg/dl allows the diagnosis of type 2 diabetes, which must be confirmed with a second dosage of glycemia and HbA1c.

Chapter 1. Type 1 and Type 2 Diabetes

Diabetes is a common disease that leads to metabolic disorders of carbohydrates and water balance.

As a result, pancreatic functions are impaired. It is the pancreas that produces an important hormone called insulin.

Insulin regulates the level of blood sugar that is supplied with food. Without it, the body cannot convert sugar into glucose, and sugar starts accumulating in the body of a person with the disease.

Apart from the pancreas disorders, the water balance is impaired as well. As a result, the tissues do not retain water, and the kidneys excrete much fluid.

What Happens When a Person Has Diabetes?

When the condition develops, the body produces too little insulin. At the same time, the level of blood sugar increases, and the cells become starved for glucose, which is the primary source of energy.

Types of Diabetes

There are two types of diabetes.

Type 1 Diabetes

This condition is also known as insulin-dependent. It usually affects young people under 40. People with type 1 diabetes will need to take insulin injections for the rest of their lives because their body produces antibodies that destroy the beta-cells which produce the hormone.

Type 1 diabetes is hard to cure. However, it is possible to restore pancreatic functions by adhering to a healthy diet. Products with a high glycemic index such as soda, juice, and sweets should be excluded.

Type 2 Diabetes

This happens as a result of the lack of sensitivity of the pancreas cells towards insulin because of the excess of nutrients. People with excess weight are the most susceptible to the disease.

Difference

	Type 1	Type 2
Whom It Affects	Represent up to 5–10 % of all cases of diabetes. It was once called "juvenile-onset" diabetes because it was thought to develop most often in children and young adults. We now know it can occur in people of any age, including older adults.	Accounts for 90–95 % of all diagnosed cases of diabetes. It used to be called "adult-onset" diabetes, but it is now known that even children—mainly if they're overweight—can develop type 2 diabetes.
What Happens	The pancreas makes little if any insulin.	The pancreas doesn't produce enough insulin or the body doesn't respond properly to the insulin that is produced.
Risk Factors	Less well-defined, but autoimmune, genetic, and environmental factors are believed to be involved.	Older age, obesity, family history of diabetes, physical inactivity, and race/ethnicity.
Treatment	Individualized meal plans, insulin therapy (usually several injections a day), self-monitoring glucose testing several times a day, regular physical activity, and a healthy diet.	A healthy diet, weight loss (if overweight), regular exercise, and monitoring blood glucose levels. Some people are able to manage blood sugar through diet and exercise alone. However, diabetes tends to be a progressive disease, so oral medications and possibly insulin may be needed at some point.

Foods to Eat

Vegetables

Fresh vegetables never cause harm to anyone. So, adding a meal full of vegetables is the best shot for all diabetic patients. But not all vegetables contain the same number of macronutrients. Some vegetables contain a high amount of carbohydrates, so those are not suitable for a diabetic diet. We need to use vegetables which contain a low amount of carbohydrates.

1. Cauliflower
2. Spinach
3. Tomatoes
4. Broccoli
5. Lemons
6. Artichoke
7. Garlic
8. Asparagus
9. Spring onions
10. Onions
11. Ginger, etc.

Meat

Meat is not on the red list for the diabetic diet. It is fine to have some meat every now and then for diabetic patients. However certain meat types are better than others. For instance, red meat is not a preferable option for such patients. They should consume white meat more often whether it's seafood or poultry. Healthy options in meat are:

1. All fish, i.e., salmon, halibut, trout, cod, sardine, etc.
2. Scallops
3. Mussels
4. Shrimp
5. Oysters, etc.

Fruits

Not all fruits are good for diabetes. To know if the fruit is suitable for this diet, it is important to note its sugar content. Some fruits contain a high number of sugars in the form of sucrose and fructose, and those should be readily avoided. Here is the list of popularly used fruits that can be taken on the diabetic diet:

1. Peaches
2. Nectarines
3. Avocados
4. Apples
5. Berries
6. Grapefruit
7. Kiwi Fruit
8. Bananas
9. Cherries
10. Grapes
11. Orange
12. Pears
13. Plums
14. Strawberries

Nuts and Seeds

Nuts and seeds are perhaps the most enriched edibles, and they contain such a mix of macronutrients that can never harm anyone. So diabetic patients can take the nuts and seeds in their diet without any fear of a glucose spike.

1. Pistachios
2. Sunflower seeds
3. Walnuts
4. Peanuts
5. Pecans
6. Pumpkin seeds
7. Almonds
8. Sesame seeds, etc.

Grains

Diabetic patients should also be selective while choosing the right grains for their diet. The idea is to keep the amount of starch as minimum as possible. That is why you won't see any white rice in the list rather it is replaced with more fibrous brown rice.

1. Quinoa
2. Oats
3. Multigrain
4. Whole grains
5. Brown rice
6. Millet
7. Barley
8. Sorghum
9. Tapioca

Fats

Fat intake is the most debated topic as far as the diabetic diet is concerned. As there are diets like ketogenic, which are loaded with fats and still proved effective for diabetic patients. The key is the absence of carbohydrates. In any other situation, fats are as harmful to diabetics as any normal person. Switching to unsaturated fats is a better option.

1. Sesame oil
2. Olive oil
3. Canola oil
4. Grapeseed oil
5. Other vegetable oils
6. Fats extracted from plant sources

Diary

Any dairy product which directly or indirectly causes a glucose rise in the blood should not be taken on this diet. Other than those, all products are good to use. These items include:

1. Skimmed milk
2. Low-fat cheese
3. Eggs
4. Yogurt
5. Trans fat-free margarine or butter

Sugar Alternatives

Since ordinary sugars or sweeteners are strictly forbidden on a diabetic diet. There are artificial varieties that can add sweetness without raising the level of carbohydrates in the meal. These substitutes are:

1. Stevia
2. Xylitol
3. Natvia

4. Swerve
5. Monk fruit
6. Erythritol

Make sure to substitute them with extra care. The sweetness of each sweetener is entirely different from the table sugar, so add each in accordance with the intensity of their flavor. Stevia is the sweetest of them, and it should be used with more care. In place of 1 c of sugar, 1 tsp of stevia is enough. All other sweeteners are more or less similar to sugar in their intensity of sweetness.

Foods to Avoid

Knowing a general scheme of diet helps a lot, but it is equally important to be well familiar with the items which have to be avoided. With this list, you can make your diet 100 % sugar-free. There are many other food items that can cause some harm to a diabetic patient as the sugars do. So, let's discuss them in some detail here.

Sugars

Sugar is a big NO-GO for a diabetic diet. Once you are diabetic, you would need to say goodbye to all the natural sweeteners which are loaded with carbohydrates. They contain polysaccharides that readily break into glucose after getting into our body. And the list does not only include table sugars but other items like honey and molasses should also be avoided.

1. White sugar
2. Brown sugar
3. Confectionary sugar
4. Honey
5. Molasses
6. Granulated sugar

Your mind and your body, will not accept the abrupt change. It is recommended to go for a gradual change. It means start substituting it with low carb substitutes in a small amount, day by day.

High Fat Dairy Products

Once you are diabetic, you may get susceptible to a number of other fatal diseases including cardiovascular ones. That is why experts strictly recommend avoiding high-fat food products, especially dairy items. The high amount of fat can make your body insulin resistant. So even when you take insulin, it won't be of any use as the body will not work on it.

Saturated Animal Fats

Saturated animal fats are not good for anyone, whether diabetic or normal. So, better avoid using them in general. Whenever you are cooking meat, try to trim off all the excess fat. Cooking oils made out of these saturated fats should be avoided. Keep yourself away from any of the animal-origin fats.

High Carb Vegetables

As discussed above, vegetables with more starch are not suitable for diabetes. These veggies can increase the carbohydrate levels of food. So, omit these from the recipes and enjoy the rest of the less starchy vegetables. Some of the high carb vegetables are:

1. Potatoes
2. Sweet potatoes
3. Yams, etc.

Cholesterol Rich Ingredients

Bad cholesterol or high-density lipoprotein has the tendency to deposit in different parts of the body. That is why food items having high bad cholesterol are not good for diabetes. Such items should be replaced with the ones with low cholesterol.

High Sodium Products

Sodium is related to hypertension and blood pressure. Since diabetes is already the result of a hormonal imbalance in the body, in the presence of excess sodium—another imbalance—a fluid imbalance may occur which a diabetic body cannot tolerate. It adds up to already present complications of the disease. So, avoid using food items with a high amount of sodium. Mainly store packed items, processed foods, and salt all contain sodium, and one should avoid them all. Use only the unsalted variety of food products, whether it's butter, margarine, nuts, or other items.

Sugary Drinks

Cola drinks or other similar beverages are filled with sugars. If you had seen different video presentations showing the amount of the sugars present in a single bottle of soda, you would know how dangerous those are for diabetic patients. They can drastically increase the amount of blood glucose level within 30 minutes of drinking. Fortunately, there are many sugar-free varieties available in the drinks which are suitable for diabetic patients.

Sugar Syrups and Toppings

A number of syrups available in the markets are made out of nothing but sugar. Maple syrup is one good example. For a diabetic diet, the patient should avoid such sugary syrups and also stay away from the sugar-rich toppings available in the stores. If you want to use them at all, trust yourself and prepare them at home with a sugar-free recipe.

Sweet Chocolate and Candies

For diabetic patients, sugar-free chocolates or candies are the best way out. Other processed chocolate bars and candies are extremely damaging to their health, and all of these should be avoided. You can try and prepare healthy bars and candies at home with sugar-free recipes.

Alcohol

Alcohol has the tendency to reduce the rate of our metabolism and take away our appetite, which can render a diabetic patient into a very life-threatening condition. Alcohol in a very small amount cannot harm the patient, but the regular or constant intake of alcohol is bad for health and glucose levels.

Chapter 3. 4-Week Meal Plan

Day	Breakfast	Lunch	Dinner	Dessert
1	Berry-oat breakfast bars	Kale, and white bean stew	Salmon with asparagus	Tuna salad
2	Whole-grain breakfast cookies	Slow cooker two-bean sloppy joes	Shrimp in garlic butter	Roasted portobello salad
3	Blueberry breakfast cake	Lighter eggplant parmesan	Cobb salad	Shredded chicken salad
4	Whole grain pancakes	Coconut-lentil curry	Seared tuna steak	Mango and jicama salad
5	Buckwheat grouts breakfast bowl	Stuffed portobello with cheese	Beef chili	Roasted beet salad
6	Peach muesli bake	Lighter shrimp scampi	Greek broccoli salad	Calico salad
7	Steel-cut oatmeal bowl with fruit and nuts	Maple-mustard salmon	Cheesy cauliflower gratin	Spinach shrimp salad
8	Whole-grain Dutch baby pancake	Chicken salad with grapes and pecans	Strawberry spinach salad	Barley veggie salad
9	Mushroom, zucchini, and onion frittata	Lemony salmon burgers	Cauliflower mac and cheese	Tenderloin grilled salad
10	Spinach and cheese quiche	Caprese turkey burgers	Easy egg salad	Broccoli salad
11	Spicy jalapeno popper deviled eggs	Pasta salad	Baked chicken legs	Broccoli salad Cherry tomato salad
12	Lovely porridge	Chicken, strawberry, and avocado salad	Creamed spinach	Tabbouleh—Arabian salad
13	Salty macadamia chocolate smoothie	Lemon-thyme eggs	Stuffed mushrooms	Arugula garden salad
14	Basil and tomato baked eggs	Spinach salad with bacon	Vegetable soup	Supreme Caesar salad
15	Cinnamon and coconut porridge	Pea and collards soup	Misto quente	Sunflower seeds and
16	An omelet of Swiss chard	Spanish stew	Garlic bread	Chicken salad in cucumber cups
17	Cheesy low-carb omelet	Creamy taco soup	Bruschetta	California wraps
18	Yogurt and kale smoothie	Chicken with Caprese salsa	Cream buns with strawberries	Chicken avocado salad
19	Bacon and chicken garlic wrap	Balsamic-roasted broccoli	Blueberry buns	Ground turkey salad

20	Grilled chicken platter	Hearty beef and vegetable soup	Cauliflower mash	Scallop Caesar salad
21	Parsley chicken breast	Cauliflower muffin	French toast in sticks	Asian cucumber salad
22	Mustard chicken	Cauliflower rice with chicken	Muffins sandwich	Cauliflower tofu salad
23	Balsamic chicken	Ham and egg cups	Bacon BBQ	Tuna salad
24	Greek chicken breast	Turkey with fried eggs	Stuffed French toast	Roasted portobello salad
25	Chipotle lettuce chicken	Kale, and white bean stew	Scallion sandwich	Shredded chicken salad
26	Stylish chicken-bacon wrap	Slow cooker two-bean sloppy joes	Lean lamb and turkey meatballs with yogurt	Mango and jicama salad
27	Healthy cottage cheese pancakes	Lighter eggplant parmesan	Air fried section and tomato	Roasted beet salad
28	Avocado lemon toast	Coconut-lentil curry	Cheesy salmon fillets	Calico salad

Chapter 4. Breakfast

1. Berry-Oat Breakfast Bars

Preparation time: 10 minutes

Servings: 12

Cooking time: 25 minutes

Ingredients:

- 2 c. fresh raspberries or blueberries
- 2 tbsps sugar
- 2 tbsps freshly squeezed lemon juice
- 1 tbsp. cornstarch
- 1 1/2 c. rolled oats
- 1/2 c. whole-wheat flour
- 1/2 c. walnuts
- 1/4 c. chia seeds
- 1/4 c. extra-virgin olive oil
- 1/4 c. honey
- 1 large egg

Directions:

1. Preheat the oven to 350 °F.
2. In a small saucepan over medium heat, stir together the berries, sugar, lemon juice, and cornstarch. Bring to a simmer. Reduce the heat and simmer for 2–3 minutes, until the mixture thickens.
3. In a food processor or high-speed blender, combine the oats, flour, walnuts, and chia seeds. Process until powdered. Add the olive oil, honey, and egg. Pulse a few more times, until well combined. Press half of the mixture into a 9-in. square baking dish.
4. Spread the berry filling over the oat mixture. Add the remaining oat mixture on top of the berries. Bake for 25 minutes, until browned.
5. Let cool completely, cut into 12 pieces, and serve. Store in a covered container for up to 5 days.

Nutrition:

- Calories 201
- Total fat 10 g.
- Saturated fat 1 g.
- Protein 5 g.
- Carbohydrates 26 g.
- Sugar 9 g.
- Fiber 5 g.
- Cholesterol 16 mg.
- Sodium 8 mg.

2. Whole-Grain Breakfast Cookies

Preparation time: 20 minutes

Servings: 18 cookies

Cooking time: 10 minutes

Ingredients:

- 2 c. rolled oats
- 1/2 c. whole-wheat flour
- 1/4 c. ground flaxseed
- 1 tsp. baking powder

- 1 c. unsweetened applesauce
- 2 large eggs
- 2 tbsps vegetable oil
- 2 tsps. vanilla extract
- 1 tsp. ground cinnamon

- 1/2 c. dried cherries
- 1/4 c. unsweetened shredded coconut
- 2 oz. dark chocolate, chopped

Directions:

1. Preheat the oven to 350 °F.
2. In a large bowl, combine the oats, flour, flaxseed, and baking powder. Stir well to mix.
3. In a medium bowl, whisk the applesauce, eggs, vegetable oil, vanilla, and cinnamon. Pour the wet mixture into the dry mixture, and stir until combined.
4. Fold in the cherries, coconut, and chocolate. Drop tablespoon-size balls of dough onto a baking sheet. Bake for 10–12 minutes, until browned and cooked through.
5. Let cool for about 3 minutes, remove from the baking sheet, and cool completely before serving. Store in an airtight container for up to 1 week.

Nutrition:

- Calories 136
- Total fat 7 g.
- Saturated fat 3 g.
- Protein 4 g.

- Carbohydrates 14 g.
- Sugar 4 g.
- Fiber 3 g.
- Cholesterol 21 mg.
- Sodium 11 mg.

3. Blueberry Breakfast Cake

Preparation time: 15 minutes

Servings: 12

Cooking time: 45 minutes

Ingredients:

For the Topping

- 1/4 c. finely chopped walnuts
- 1/2 tsp. ground cinnamon
- 2 tbsps butter, chopped into small pieces
- 2 tbsps sugar

- 1 c. whole-wheat pastry flour
- 1 c. oat flour
- 1/4 c. sugar
- 2 tsps. baking powder
- 1 large egg, beaten
- 1/2 c. skim milk
- 2 tbsps butter, melted
- 1 tsp. grated lemon peel
- 2 c. fresh or frozen blueberries

For the Cake

- Nonstick cooking spray

Directions:

To Make the Topping

1. In a small bowl, stir together the walnuts, cinnamon, butter, and sugar. Set aside.

To Make the Cake

1. Preheat the oven to 350 °F. Spray a 9-in. square pan with cooking spray. Set aside.
2. In a large bowl, stir together the pastry flour, oat flour, sugar, and baking powder.
3. Add the egg, milk, butter, and lemon peel, and stir until there are no dry spots.
4. Stir in the blueberries, and gently mix until incorporated. Press the batter into the prepared pan, using a spoon to flatten it into the dish.
5. Sprinkle the topping over the cake.
6. Bake for 40–45 minutes until a toothpick inserted into the cake comes out clean and serve.

Nutrition:

- Calories 177
- Total fat 7 g.
- Saturated fat 3 g.
- Protein 4 g.
- Carbohydrates 26 g.
- Sugar 9 g.
- Fiber 3 g.
- Cholesterol 26 mg.
- Sodium 39 mg.

4. Whole-Grain Pancakes

Preparation time: 10 minutes

Servings: 4–6

Cooking time: 15 minutes

Ingredients:

- 2 c. whole-wheat pastry flour
- 4 tsps. baking powder
- 2 tsps. ground cinnamon
- 1/2 tsp. salt
- 2 c. skim milk, plus more as needed
- 2 large eggs
- 1 tbsp. honey
- Nonstick cooking spray
- Maple syrup, for serving
- Fresh fruit, for serving

Directions:

1. In a large bowl, stir together the flour, baking powder, cinnamon, and salt.
2. Add the milk, eggs, and honey, and stir well to combine. If needed, add more milk, 1 tbsp. at a time, until there are no dry spots and you have a pourable batter.
3. Heat a large skillet over medium-high heat, and spray it with cooking spray.
4. Using a 1/4-cup measuring cup, scoop 2 or 3 pancakes into the skillet at a time. Cook for a couple of minutes, until bubbles form on the surface of the pancakes, flip, and cook for 1–2 minutes more, until golden brown and cooked through. Repeat with the remaining batter.
5. Serve topped with maple syrup or fresh fruit.

Nutrition:

- Calories 392
- Total fat 4 g.
- Saturated fat 1 g.
- Protein 15 g.
- Carbohydrates 71 g.
- Sugar 11 g.
- Fiber 9 g.
- Cholesterol 95 mg.
- Sodium 396 mg.

5. Buckwheat Grouts Breakfast Bowl

Preparation time: 5 minutes, plus overnight to   soak

Cooking time: 10–12 minutes

Servings: 4

Ingredients:

- 3 c. skim milk
- 1 c. buckwheat grouts
- 1/4 c. chia seeds
- 2 tsps. vanilla extract
- 1/2 tsp. ground cinnamon
-)
- Pinch salt
- 1 c. water
- 1/2 c. unsalted pistachios
- 2 c. sliced fresh strawberries
- 1/4 c. cacao nibs (optional

Directions:

1. In a large bowl, stir together the milk, groats, chia seeds, vanilla, cinnamon, and salt. Cover and refrigerate overnight.
2. The next morning, transfer the soaked mixture to a medium pot and add the water. Bring to a boil over medium-high heat, reduce the heat to maintain a simmer, and cook for 10–12 minutes, until the buckwheat is tender and thickened.
3. Transfer to bowls and serve, topped with the pistachios, strawberries, and cacao nibs (if using).

Nutrition:

- Calories 340
- Total fat 8 g.
- Saturated fat 1 g.
- Protein 15 g.
- Carbohydrates 52 g.
- Sugar 14 g.
- Fiber 10 g.
- Cholesterol 4 mg.
- Sodium 140 mg.

6. Peach Muesli Bake

Preparation time: 10 minutes

Servings: 8

Cooking time: 40 minutes

Ingredients:

- Nonstick cooking spray
- 2 c. skim milk
- 1 1/2 c. rolled oats
- 1/2 c. chopped walnuts
- 1 large egg
- 2 tbsps maple syrup
- 1 tsp. ground cinnamon
- 1 tsp. baking powder
- 1/2 tsp. salt
- 2–3 peaches, sliced

Directions:

1. Preheat the oven to 375 °F. Spray a 9-in. square baking dish with cooking spray. Set aside.
2. In a large bowl, stir together the milk, oats, walnuts, egg, maple syrup, cinnamon, baking powder, and salt. Spread half the mixture in the prepared baking dish.
3. Place half the peaches in a single layer across the oat mixture.

4. Spread the remaining oat mixture over the top. Add the remaining peaches in a thin layer over the oats. Bake for 35–40 minutes, uncovered until thickened and browned.
5. Cut into 8 squares and serve warm.

Nutrition:

- Calories 138
- Total fat 3 g.
- Saturated fat 1 g.
- Protein 6 g.
- Carbohydrates 22 g.
- Sugar 10 g.
- Fiber 3 g.
- Cholesterol 24 mg.
- Sodium 191 mg.

7. Steel-Cut Oatmeal Bowl with Fruit and Nuts

Preparation time: 5 minutes

Cooking time: 20 minutes

Servings: 4

Ingredients:

- 1 c. steel-cut oats
- 2 c. almond milk
- 3/4 c. water
- 1 tsp. ground cinnamon
- 1/4 tsp. salt
- 2 c. chopped fresh fruit, such as blueberries, strawberries, raspberries, or peaches
- 1/2 c. chopped walnuts
- 1/4 c. chia seeds

Directions:

1. In a medium saucepan over medium-high heat, combine the oats, almond milk, water, cinnamon, and salt. Bring to a boil, reduce the heat to low, and simmer for 15-20 minutes, until the oats are softened and thickened.
2. Top each bowl with 1/2 c of fresh fruit, 2 tbsps of walnuts, and 1 tbsp of chia seeds before serving.

Nutrition:

- Calories 288
- Total fat 11 g.
- Saturated fat 1 g.
- Protein 10 g.
- Carbohydrates 38 g.
- Sugar 7 g.
- Fiber 10 g.
- Cholesterol 0 mg.
- Sodium 329 mg.

8. Whole-Grain Dutch Baby Pancake

Preparation time: 5 minutes

Servings: 4

Cooking time: 25 minutes

Ingredients:

- 2 tbsps coconut oil
- 1/2 c. whole-wheat flour
- 1/4 c. skim milk
- 3 large eggs

- 1 tsp. vanilla extract
- 1/2 tsp. baking powder
- 1/4 tsp. salt
- 1/4 tsp. ground cinnamon
- Powdered sugar, for dusting

Directions:

1. Preheat the oven to 400 °F.
2. Put the coconut oil in a medium oven-safe skillet, and place the skillet in the oven to melt the oil while it preheats.
3. In a blender, combine the flour, milk, eggs, vanilla, baking powder, salt, and cinnamon. Process until smooth.
4. Carefully remove the skillet from the oven and tilt to spread the oil around evenly.
5. Pour the batter into the skillet and return it to the oven for 23–25 minutes, until the pancake puffs and lightly browns.
6. Remove, dust lightly with powdered sugar, cut into 4 wedges, and serve.

Nutrition:

- Calories 195
- Total fat 11 g.
- Saturated fat 7 g.
- Protein 8 g.

- Carbohydrates 16 g.
- Sugar 1 g.
- Fiber 2 g.
- Cholesterol 140 mg.
- Sodium 209 mg.

9. Mushroom, Zucchini, and Onion Frittata

Preparation time: 10 minutes   **Servings:** 4

Cooking time: 20 minutes

Ingredients:

- 1 tbsp. extra-virgin olive oil
- 1/2 onion, chopped
- 1 medium zucchini, chopped
- 1 1/2 c. sliced mushrooms

- 6 large eggs, beaten
- 2 tbsps skim milk
- Salt
- Freshly ground black pepper
- 1-oz. feta cheese, crumbled

Directions:

1. Preheat the oven to 400 °F.
2. In a medium oven-safe skillet over medium-high heat, heat the olive oil.
3. Add the onion and sauté for 3–5 minutes, until translucent.
4. Add the zucchini and mushrooms, and cook for 3–5 more minutes, until the vegetables are tender.
5. Meanwhile, in a small bowl, whisk the eggs, milk, salt, and pepper. Pour the mixture into the skillet, stirring to combine, and transfer the skillet to the oven. Cook for 7–9 minutes, until set.
6. Sprinkle with the feta cheese, and cook for 1–2 minutes more, until heated through.

7. Remove, cut into 4 wedges, and serve.

Nutrition:

- Calories 178
- Total fat 13 g.
- Saturated fat 4 g.
- Protein 12 g.
- Carbohydrates 5 g.
- Sugar 3 g.
- Fiber 1 g.
- Cholesterol 285 mg.
- Sodium 234 mg.

10.   Spinach and Cheese Quiche

Preparation time: 10 minutes, plus 10 minutes to rest

Cooking time: 50 minutes

Servings: 4–6

Ingredients:

- Nonstick cooking spray
- 1 tbsp. + 2 tsps. extra-virgin olive oil, divided
- 1/2 tsp. salt
- Freshly ground black pepper
- 1 onion, finely chopped
- 1 (10-oz.) bag fresh spinach
- 4 large eggs
- 1/2 c. skim milk
- 1-oz. Gruyere cheese, shredded

Directions:

1. Preheat the oven to 350 °F. Spray a 9-in. pie dish with cooking spray. Set aside.
2. In a large skillet over medium-high heat, heat olive oil.
3. Add the onion and sauté for 3–5 minutes, until softened.
4. By handfuls, add the spinach, stirring between each addition, until it just starts to wilt before adding more. Cook for about 1 minute, until it cooks down.
5. In a medium bowl, whisk the eggs and milk. Add the gruyere, and season with salt and some pepper. Fold the eggs into the spinach. Pour the mixture into the pie dish and bake for 25 minutes, until the eggs are set.
6. Let rest for 10 minutes before serving.

Nutrition:

- Calories 445
- Total fat 14 g.
- Saturated fat 4 g.
- Protein 19 g.
- Carbohydrates 68 g.
- Sugar 6 g.
- Fiber 7 g.
- Cholesterol 193 mg.
- Sodium 773 mg.

11. Spicy Jalapeno Popper Deviled Eggs

Preparation time: 5 minutes

Cooking time: 5 minutes

Servings: 4

Ingredients:

- 4 large whole eggs, hardboiled
- 2 tbsps keto-friendly mayonnaise

- 1/4 c. cheddar cheese, grated
- 2 slices bacon, cooked and crumbled
- 1 jalapeno, sliced

Directions:

1. Cut eggs in half, remove the yolk, and put them in a bowl.
2. Lay egg whites on a platter.
3. Mix in the remaining ingredients and mash them with the egg yolks.
4. Transfer the yolk mixture back to the egg whites.
5. Serve and enjoy!

Nutrition:

- Calories 176
- Fat 14 g.

- Carbohydrates 0.7 g.
- Protein 10 g.

12.   Lovely Porridge

Preparation time: 15 minutes

Servings: 2

Cooking time: Nil

Ingredients:

- 2 tbsps coconut flour
- 2 tbsps vanilla protein powder

- 3 tbsps Golden Flaxseed meal
- 1 1/2 c. almond milk, unsweetened
- Powdered erythritol

Directions:

1. Take a bowl and mix with flaxseed meal, protein powder, coconut flour, and mix well.
2. Add the mix to the saucepan (placed over medium heat).
3. Add almond milk and stir, let the mixture thicken.
4. Add your desired amount of sweetener and serve.
5. Enjoy!

Nutrition:

- Calories 259
- Fat 13 g.
- Carbohydrates 5 g.
- Protein 16 g.

Chapter 5. Lunch

13. Cauliflower Rice with Chicken

Preparation time: 15 minutes

Cooking time: 15 minutes

Ingredients:

- 1/2 large cauliflower
- 3/4 c. cooked meat
- 1/2 bell pepper
- 1 carrot
- 2 ribs celery
- 1 tbsp. stir fry sauce (low carb)
-

Servings: 4

- 1 tbsp. extra-virgin olive oil
- Salt and pepper to taste

Directions:

1. Chop cauliflower in a processor to "rice." Place in a bowl.
2. Properly chop all vegetables in a food processor into thin slices.
3. Add cauliflower and other plants to a wok with heated oil. Fry until all veggies are tender.
4. Add chopped meat and sauce to the wok and fry for 10 minutes.
5. Serve.

This dish is very mouth-watering!

Nutrition:

- Calories 200
- Protein 10 g.
- Fat 12 g.
- Carbohydrates 10 g.

14. Turkey with Fried Eggs

Preparation time: 10 minutes

Cooking time: 20 minutes

Ingredients:

- 1 cooked turkey thigh
- 1 large onion (about 2 c. diced)
- Butter

Servings: 4

- Chile flakes
- 4 eggs

- Salt to taste
- Pepper to taste

Directions:

1. Dice the turkey.
2. Cook the onion in as much unsalted butter as you feel comfortable with until it's fragrant and translucent.
3. Add 1 c of diced cooked turkey, salt, and pepper to taste, and cook for 20 minutes.
4. Top each with a fried egg. Yummy!

Nutrition:

- Fat 7 g.
- Carbohydrates 6 g.
- Calories 170
- Protein 19 g.

15.   Kale and White Bean Stew

Preparation time: 15 minutes

Cooking time: 25 minutes

Servings: 4

Ingredients:

- 1 (15-oz.) can low-sodium cannellini beans, rinsed and drained, divided
- 1 tbsp. olive oil
- 1 medium onion, chopped
- 2 garlic cloves, minced
- 2 celery stalks, chopped
- 3 medium carrots, chopped
- 2 c. low-sodium vegetable broth
- 1 tsp. apple cider vinegar
- 2 c. chopped kale
- 1 c. shelled edamame
- 1/4 c. quinoa
- 1 tsp. dried thyme
- 1/2 tsp. cayenne pepper
- 1/2 tsp. salt
- 1/4 tsp. freshly ground black pepper

Directions:

1. Put half the beans into a blender and blend until smooth. Set aside.
2. In a large soup pot over medium heat, heat the oil. When the oil is shining, include the onion and garlic, and cook until the onion softens and the garlic is sweet, for about 3 minutes. Add the celery and carrots, and continue cooking until the vegetables soften, for about 5 minutes.
3. Add the broth, vinegar, unblended beans, kale, edamame, and quinoa, and bring the mixture to a boil. Reduce the heat and simmer until the vegetables soften, for about 10 minutes.
4. Add the blended beans, thyme, cayenne, salt, and black pepper, increase the heat to medium-high, and bring the mixture to a boil. Reduce the heat and simmer, uncovered, until the flavors combine, for about 5 minutes.
5. Into each of 4 containers, scoop 1 3/4 cups of stew.

Nutrition:

- Calories 373
- Total fat 7 g.
- Saturated fat 1 g.
- Protein 15 g.
- Total carbs 65 g.
- Fiber 15 g.
- Sugar 13 g.
- Sodium 540 mg.

16. Slow Cooker Two-Bean Sloppy Joes

Preparation time: 10 minutes

Cooking time: 6 hours

Servings: 4

Ingredients:

- 1 (15-oz.) can of low-sodium black beans
- 1 (15-oz.) can of low-sodium pinto beans
- 1 (15-oz.) can of no-salt-added diced tomatoes
- 1 medium green bell pepper, cored, seeded, and chopped
- 1 medium yellow onion, chopped
- 1/4 c. low-sodium vegetable broth
- 2 garlic cloves, minced
- 2 servings (1/4 c.) meal prep barbecue sauce or bottled barbecue sauce
- 1/4 tsp. salt
- 1/4 tsp. freshly ground black pepper
- 4 whole-wheat buns

Directions:

1. In a slow cooker, combine the black beans, pinto beans, diced tomatoes, bell pepper, onion, broth, garlic, meal prep barbecue sauce, salt, and black pepper. Stir the ingredients, then cover and cook on low for 6 hours.
2. Into each of 4 containers, spoon 1 1/4 c of sloppy joe mix. Serve with 1 whole-wheat bun.
3. Storage: place airtight containers in the refrigerator for up to 1 week. To freeze, place freezer-safe containers in the freezer for up to 2 months. To defrost, refrigerate overnight. To reheat individual portions, microwave uncovered on high for 2–2 1/2 minutes. Alternatively, reheat the entire dish in a saucepan on the stovetop. Bring the sloppy joes to a boil, then reduce the heat and simmer until heated through, for 10–15 minutes. Serve with a whole-wheat bun.

Nutrition:

- Calories 392
- Total fat 3 g.
- Saturated fat 0 g.
- Protein 17 g.
- Total carbs 79 g.
- Fiber 19 g.
- Sugar 15 g.
- Sodium 759 mg.

17. Lighter Eggplant Parmesan

Preparation time: 15 minutes

Cooking time: 35 minutes

Servings: 4

Ingredients:

- Nonstick cooking spray
- 3 eggs, beaten
- 1 tbsp. dried parsley
- 2 tsps. ground oregano
- 1/8 tsp. freshly ground black pepper

- 1 c. panko bread crumbs, preferably whole-wheat
- 1 large eggplant (about 2 lbs.)
- 5 servings (2 1/2 c.) chunky tomato sauce or jarred low-sodium tomato sauce

- 1 c. part-skim mozzarella cheese
- 1/4 c. grated parmesan cheese

Directions:

1. Preheat the oven to 450 °F. Coat a baking sheet with cooking spray.
2. In a medium bowl, whisk together the eggs, parsley, oregano, and pepper.
3. Pour the panko into a separate medium bowl.
4. Slice the eggplant into 1/4-in.-thick slices. Dip each slice of eggplant into the egg mixture, shaking off the excess. Then dredge both sides of the eggplant in the panko bread crumbs. Place the coated eggplant on the prepared baking sheet, leaving a 1/2-in. space between each slice.
5. Bake for about 15 minutes until soft and golden brown. Remove from the oven and set aside to slightly cool.
6. Pour 1/2 c of chunky tomato sauce on the bottom of an 8-by-15-in. baking dish. Using a spatula or the back of a spoon spread the tomato sauce evenly. Place half the slices of the cooked eggplant, slightly overlapping, in the dish, and top with 1 c of chunky tomato sauce, 1/2 c of mozzarella, and 2 tbsps of grated parmesan. Repeat the layer, ending with the cheese.
7. Bake uncovered for 20 minutes until the cheese is bubbling and slightly browned.
8. Remove from the oven and allow cooling for 15 minutes before dividing the eggplant equally into 4 separate containers.

Nutrition:

- Calories 333
- Total fat 14 g.
- Saturated fat 6 g.
- Protein 20 g.

- Total carbs 35 g.
- Fiber 11 g.
- Sugar 15 g.
- Sodium 994 mg.

18.   Coconut-Lentil Curry

Preparation time: 15 minutes

Servings: 4

Cooking time: 35 minutes

Ingredients:

- 1 tbsp. olive oil
- 1 medium yellow onion, chopped
- 1 garlic clove, minced
- 1 medium red bell pepper, diced
- 1 (15-oz.) can green or brown lentils, rinsed and drained
- 1 (15-oz.) can no-salt-added diced tomatoes

- 2 tbsps tomato paste
- 4 tsps. curry powder
- 1/8 tsp. ground cloves
- 1 (15-oz.) can light coconut milk
- 1/4 tsp. salt
- 2 pieces' whole-wheat naan bread, halved, or 4 slices crusty bread

Directions:

1. In a large saucepan over medium heat, heat the olive oil. When the oil is shimmering, add both the onion and garlic and cook until the onion softens and the garlic is sweet, for about 3 minutes.

2. Add the bell pepper and continue cooking until it softens, about 5 minutes more. Add the lentils, tomatoes, tomato paste, curry powder, and cloves, and bring the mixture to a boil. Reduce the heat to medium-low, cover, and simmer
3. Add the coconut milk and salt, and return to a boil. Reduce the heat and simmer until the flavors combine, for about 5 minutes.
4. Into each of 4 containers, spoon 2 c of curry.
5. Enjoy each serving with half of a piece of naan bread or 1 slice of crusty bread.

Nutrition:

- Calories 559
- Total fat 16 g.
- Saturated fat 7 g.
- Protein 16 g.
- Total carbs 86 g.
- Fiber 16 g.
- Sugar 18 g.
- Sodium 819 mg.

19.   Stuffed Portobello with Cheese

Preparation time: 15 minutes

Cooking time: 25 minutes

Servings: 4

Ingredients:

- 4 portobello mushroom caps
- 1 tbsp. olive oil
- 1/2 tsp. salt, divided
- 1/4 tsp. freshly ground black pepper, divided
- 1 c. baby spinach, chopped
- 1 1/2 c. part-skim ricotta cheese
- 1/2 c. part-skim shredded mozzarella cheese
- 1/4 c. grated parmesan cheese
- 1 garlic clove, minced
- 1 tbsp. dried parsley
- 2 tsps. dried oregano
- 4 tsps. unseasoned bread crumbs, divided
- 4 servings (4 c.) roasted broccoli with shallots

Directions:

1. Preheat the oven to 375 °F. Line a baking sheet with aluminum foil.
2. Brush the mushroom caps with olive oil, and sprinkle with 1/4 tsp. salt and 1/8 tsp. pepper. Put the mushroom caps on the prepared baking sheet and bake until soft, about 12 minutes.
3. In a medium bowl, mix together the spinach, ricotta, mozzarella, parmesan, garlic, parsley, oregano, and the remaining 1/4 tsp of salt and 1/8 tsp of pepper.
4. Spoon 1/2 c of cheese mixture into each mushroom cap, and sprinkle each with 1 tsp of bread crumbs. Return the mushrooms to the oven for an additional 8–10 minutes until warmed through.
5. Remove from the oven and allow the mushrooms to cool for about 10 minutes before placing each in an individual container. Add 1 c of roasted broccoli with shallots to each container.

Nutrition:

- Calories 419
- Total fat 30 g.
- Saturated fat 10 g.
- Protein 23 g.
- Total carbs 19 g.
- Fiber 2 g.
- Sugar 3 g.
- Sodium 790 mg.

20.   Lighter Shrimp Scampi

Preparation time: 15 minutes

Servings: 4

Cooking time: 15 minutes

Ingredients:

- 1 1/2 lbs. large peeled and deveined shrimp
- 1/4 tsp. salt
- 1/8 tsp. freshly ground black pepper
- 2 tbsps olive oil
- 1 shallot, chopped
- 2 garlic cloves, minced
- 1/4 c. cooking white wine
- Juice of 1/2 lemon (1 tbsp.)
- 1/2 tsp. sriracha
- 2 tbsps unsalted butter, at room temperature
- 1/4 c. chopped fresh parsley
- 4 servings (6 c.) zucchini noodles with lemon vinaigrette

Directions:

1. Season the shrimp with salt and pepper.
2. In a medium saucepan over medium heat, heat the oil. Add the shallot and garlic, and cook until the shallot softens and the garlic is fragrant, for about 3 minutes. Add the shrimp, cover, and cook until opaque, 2–3 minutes on each side. Using a slotted spoon, transfer the shrimp to a large plate.
3. Add the wine, lemon juice, and sriracha to the saucepan, and stir to combine. Bring the mixture to a boil, then reduce the heat and simmer until the liquid is reduced by about half, 3 minutes. Add the butter and stir until melted, about 3 minutes. Return the shrimp to the saucepan and toss to coat. Add the parsley and stir to combine.
4. Into each of 4 containers, place 1 1/2 c of zucchini noodles with lemon vinaigrette, and top with 3/4 c of scampi.

Nutrition:

- Calories 364
- Total fat 21 g.
- Saturated fat 6 g.
- Protein 37 g.
- Total carbs 10 g.
- Fiber 2 g.
- Sugar 6 g.
- Sodium 557 mg.

21.   Maple-Mustard Salmon

Preparation time: 10 minutes, plus 30 minutes marinating time

Servings: 4

Cooking time: 20 minutes

Ingredients:

- Nonstick cooking spray
- 1/2 c. 100 % maple syrup
- 2 tbsps Dijon mustard
- 1/4 tsp. salt
- 4 (5-oz.) salmon fillets
- 4 servings (4 c.) roasted broccoli with shallots
- 4 servings (2 c.) parleyed whole-wheat couscous

Directions:

1. Preheat the oven to 400 °F. Line a baking sheet with aluminum foil and coat with cooking spray.
2. In a medium bowl, whisk together the maple syrup, mustard, and salt until smooth.
3. Put the salmon fillets into the bowl and toss to coat. Cover and place in the refrigerator to marinate for at least 30 minutes and up to overnight.
4. Shake off excess marinade from the salmon fillets and place them on the prepared baking sheet, leaving a 1-in. space between each fillet. Discard the extra marinade.
5. Bake for about 20 minutes until the salmon is opaque and a thermometer inserted in the thickest part of a fillet reads 145 °F.
6. Into each of 4 resealable containers, place 1 salmon fillet, 1 c of roasted broccoli with shallots, and 1/2 c of parleyed whole-wheat couscous.

Nutrition:

- Calories 601
- Total fat 29 g.
- Saturated fat 4 g.
- Protein 36 g.
- Total carbs 51 g.
- Fiber 3 g.
- Sugar 23 g.
- Sodium 610 mg.

22. Chicken Salad with Grapes and Pecans

Preparation time: 15 minutes

Cooking time: 5 minutes

Servings: 4

Ingredients:

- 1/3 c. unsalted pecans, chopped
- 10 oz. cooked skinless, boneless chicken breast or rotisserie chicken, finely chopped
- 1/2 medium yellow onion, finely chopped
- 1 celery stalk, finely chopped
- 3/4 c. red or green seedless grapes, halved
- 1/4 c. light mayonnaise
- 1/4 c. nonfat plain Greek yogurt
- 1 tbsp. Dijon mustard
- 1 tbsp. dried parsley
- 1/4 tsp. salt
- 1/8 tsp. freshly ground black pepper
- 1 c. shredded romaine lettuce
- 4 (8-in.) whole-wheat pitas

Directions:

1. Heat a small skillet over medium-low heat to toast the pecans. Cook the pecans until fragrant, about 3 minutes. Remove from the heat and set aside to cool.
2. In a medium bowl, mix the chicken, onion, celery, pecans, and grapes.
3. In a small bowl, whisk together the mayonnaise, yogurt, mustard, parsley, salt, and pepper. Spoon the sauce over the chicken mixture and stir until well combined.
4. Into each of 4 containers, place 1/4 c of lettuce and top with 1 c of chicken salad. Store the pitas separately until ready to serve.
5. When ready to eat, stuff the serving of salad and lettuce into 1 pita.

Nutrition:

- Calories 418
- Total fat 14 g.
- Saturated fat 2 g.
- Protein 31 g.
- Total carbs 43 g.
- Fiber 6 g.

23. Roasted Vegetables

Preparation time: 14 minutes

Servings: 3

Cooking time: 17 minutes

Ingredients:

- 4 tbsp. olive oil, reserve some for greasing
- 2 heads, large garlic, tops sliced off
- 2 large eggplants/aubergines, tops removed, cubed
- 2 large shallots, peeled, quartered
- 1 large carrot, peeled, cubed
- 1 large parsnip, peeled, cubed

-

- 1/2 tsp. rosemary leaves
- 1 small green bell pepper, deseeded, ribbed, cubed
- 1 small red bell pepper, deseeded, ribbed, cubed
- 1/2 lb. Brussels sprouts, halved, do not remove cores
- 1 sprig, large thyme, leaves picked
- Sea salt, coarse-grained

For garnish

- 1 large lemon, halved, 1/2 squeezed, 1/2 sliced into smaller wedges

- 1/8 c. fennel bulb, minced

Directions:

1. From 425 °F or 220°C preheat the oven for at least 5 minutes before using.
2. Line deep roasting pan with aluminum foil; lightly grease with oil. Tumble in bell peppers, Brussels sprouts, carrots, eggplants, garlic, parsnips, rosemary leaves, shallots, and thyme. Add a pinch of sea salt; drizzle in remaining oil and lemon juice. Toss well to combine.
3. Cover roasting pan with a sheet of aluminum foil. Place this on the middle rack of the oven. Bake for 20–30 minutes. Remove aluminum foil. Roast, for another 5–10 minutes, or until the vegetables are brown at the edges. Remove roasting pan from oven. Cool slightly before ladling equal portions into plates.
4. Garnish with fennel and a wedge of lemon. Squeeze lemon juice on top of the dish before eating.

Nutrition:

- Calories 163
- Total fat 4.2 g.
- Saturated fat 0.8 g.
- Cholesterol 0 mg.

- Sodium 861 mg.
- Total carbs 22.5 g.
- Fiber 6.3 g.
- Sugar 2.3 g.
- Protein 9.2 g.

24. Millet Pilaf

Preparation time: 10 minutes

Cooking time: 15 minutes

Servings: 4

Ingredients:

- 1 c. millet
- 2 tomatoes, rinsed, seeded, and chopped
- 1 3/4 cups filtered water
- 2 tbsps extra-virgin olive oil
- 1/4 c. chopped dried apricot
- Zest of 1 lemon
- Juice of 1 lemon
- 1/2 c. fresh parsley, rinsed and chopped
- Himalayan pink salt
- Freshly ground black pepper

Directions:

1. In an electric pressure cooker, combine the millet, tomatoes, and water. Lock the lid into place, select Manual and High Pressure, and cook for 7 minutes.
2. When the beep sounds, quick release the pressure by pressing Cancel and twisting the steam valve to the Venting position. Carefully remove the lid.
3. Stir in olive oil, apricot, lemon zest, lemon juice, and parsley. Taste, season with salt and pepper and serve.

Nutrition:

- Calories 270
- Total fat 8 g.
- Total carbohydrates 42 g.
- Fiber 5 g.
- Sugar 3 g.
- Protein 6 g.

Chapter 6. Dinner

25. Cauliflower Mac and Cheese

Preparation time: 5 minutes

Cooking time: 25 minutes

Servings: 4

Ingredients:

- 1 cauliflower head, torn into florets
- Salt and black pepper, as needed
- 1/4 c. almond milk, unsweetened
- 1/4 c. heavy cream
- 3 tbsp. butter, preferably grass-fed
- 1 c. cheddar cheese, shredded
-

Directions:

1. Preheat the oven to 450 °F.
2. Melt the butter in a small microwave-safe bowl and heat it for 30 seconds.
3. Pour the melted butter over the cauliflower florets along with salt and pepper. Toss them well.
4. Place the cauliflower florets in a parchment paper-covered large baking sheet.
5. Bake them for 15 minutes or until the cauliflower is crisp-tender.
6. Once baked, mix the heavy cream, cheddar cheese, almond milk, and the remaining butter in a large microwave-safe bowl and heat it on high heat for 2 minutes or until the cheese mixture is smooth. Repeat the procedure until the cheese has melted.
7. Finally, stir in the cauliflower to the sauce mixture and coat well.

Nutrition:

- Calories 294
- Fat 23 g.
- Carbohydrates 7 g.
- Proteins 11 g.

26. Easy Egg Salad

Preparation time: 5 minutes

Cooking time: 15–20 minutes

Servings: 4

Ingredients:

- 6 eggs, preferably free-range
- 1/4 tsp. salt
- 2 tbsp. mayonnaise

- 1 tsp. lemon juice
- 1 tsp. Dijon mustard
- Pepper, to taste
- Lettuce leaves, to serve

Directions:

1. Keep the eggs in a saucepan of water and pour cold water until it covers the egg by another 1 in.
2. Bring to a boil and then remove the eggs from heat.
3. Peel the eggs under cold running water.
4. Transfer the cooked eggs into a food processor and pulse them until chopped.
5. Stir in the mayonnaise, lemon juice, salt, Dijon mustard, pepper and mix them well.
6. Taste for seasoning and add more if required.
7. Serve in the lettuce leaves.

Nutrition:

- Calories 166
- Fat 14 g.

- Carbohydrates - 0.85 g.
- Proteins 10 g.
- Sodium 132 mg.

27. Baked Chicken Legs

Preparation time: 10 minutes

Cooking time: 40 minutes

Servings: 6

- 1/4 tsp. black pepper
- 1/4 c. butter
- 1/2 tsp. sea salt
- 1/2 tsp. smoked paprika
- 1/2 tsp. garlic powder

Ingredients:

- 6 chicken legs

Directions:

1. Preheat the oven to 425 °F.
2. Pat the chicken legs with a paper towel to absorb any excess moisture.
3. Marinate the chicken pieces by first applying the butter over them and then with the seasoning. Set it aside for a few minutes.
4. Bake them for 25 minutes. Turnover and bake for further 10 minutes or until the internal temperature reaches 165 °F.
5. Serve them hot.

Nutrition:

- Calories 236

- Fat 16 g.

- Carbohydrates 0 g.

- Protein 22 g.
- Sodium 314 mg.

28. Creamed Spinach

Preparation time: 5 minutes

Cooking time: 10 minutes

Ingredients:

Servings: 4

- 1/2 c. heavy cream
- 3 oz. cream cheese

- 3 tbsp. butter
- 1/4 tsp. black pepper
- 4 cloves of garlic, minced
- 1/4 tsp. sea salt
- 10 oz. baby spinach, chopped
- 1 tsp. Italian seasoning

Directions:

1. Melt butter in a large sauté pan over medium heat.
2. Once the butter has melted, spoon in the garlic and sauté for 30 seconds or until aromatic.
3. Spoon in the spinach and cook for 3–4 minutes or until wilted.
4. Add all the remaining ingredients to it and continuously stir until the cream cheese melts and the mixture gets thickened.
5. Serve hot.

Nutrition:

- Calories 274
- Fat 27 g.

- Carbohydrates 4 g.
- Protein 4 g.
- Sodium 114 mg.

29. Stuffed Mushrooms

Preparation time: 10 minutes

Cooking time: 20 minutes

Servings: 4

Ingredients:

- 4 portobello mushrooms, large
- 1/2 c. mozzarella cheese, shredded
- 1/2 c. marinara, low-sugar
- Olive oil spray

Directions:

1. Preheat the oven to 375 °F.
2. Take out the dark gills from the mushrooms with the help of a spoon.
3. Keep the mushroom stem upside down and spoon it with 2 tbsps of marinara sauce and mozzarella cheese.
4. Bake for 18 minutes or until the cheese is bubbly.

Nutrition:

- Calories 113
- Fat 6 g.
- Carbohydrates 4 g.
- Protein 7 g.
- Sodium 14 mg.

30. Vegetable Soup

Preparation time: 10 minutes

Cooking time: 30 minutes

Servings: 5

Ingredients:

- 8 c. vegetable broth
- 2 tbsp. olive oil
- 1 tbsp. Italian seasoning
- 1 onion, large and diced
- 2 bay leaves, dried
- 2 bell pepper, large and diced
- Sea salt and black pepper, as needed
- 4 cloves of garlic, minced

- 28 oz. tomatoes, diced
- 1 cauliflower head, medium and torn into florets
- 2 c. green beans, trimmed and chopped

Directions:

1. Heat oil in a Dutch oven over medium heat.
2. Once the oil becomes hot, stir in the onions and pepper.
3. Cook for 10 minutes or until the onion is softened and browned.
4. Spoon in the garlic and sauté for a minute or until fragrant.
5. Add all the remaining ingredients to it. Mix until everything comes together.
6. Bring the mixture to a boil. Lower the heat and cook for further 20 minutes or until the vegetables have softened.
7. Serve hot.

Nutrition:

- Calories 79
- Fat 2 g.
- Carbohydrates 8 g.
- Protein 2 g.
- Sodium 187 mg.

31.   Pork Chop Diane

Preparation time: 10 minutes   **Servings:** 4

Cooking time: 20 minutes

Ingredients:

- 1/4 c. low-sodium chicken broth
- 1 tbsp. freshly squeezed lemon juice
- 2 tsps. Worcestershire sauce
- 2 tsps. Dijon mustard

- 4 (5-oz.) boneless pork top loin chops
- 1 tsp. extra-virgin olive oil
- 1 tsp. lemon zest
- 1 tsp. butter
- 2 tsps. chopped fresh chives

Directions:

1. Blend together the chicken broth, lemon juice, Worcestershire sauce, and Dijon mustard and set it aside.
2. Season the pork chops lightly.
3. Situate a large skillet over medium-high heat and add the olive oil.
4. Cook the pork chops, turning once, until they are no longer pink, about 8 minutes per side.
5. Put aside the chops.
6. Pour the broth mixture into the skillet and cook until warmed through and thickened, about 2 minutes.
7. Blend lemon zest, butter, and chives.
8. Garnish with a generous spoonful of sauce.

Nutrition:

- Calories 200

- Fat 8 g.
- Carbohydrates 1 g.

32.   Autumn Pork Chops with Red Cabbage and Apples

Preparation time: 15 minutes   **Servings:** 4

Cooking time: 30 minutes

Ingredients:

- 1/4 c. apple cider vinegar
- 2 tbsps granulated sweetener
- 4 (4-oz.) pork chops, about 1 in. thick
- 1 tbsp. extra-virgin olive oil

- 1/2 red cabbage, finely shredded
- 1 sweet onion, thinly sliced
- 1 apple, peeled, cored, and sliced
- 1 tsp. chopped fresh thyme
- Salt and pepper, to taste

Directions:

1. Mix vinegar and sweetener. Set it aside.
2. Season the pork with salt and pepper.
3. Position a big skillet over medium-high heat and add the olive oil.
4. Cook the pork chops until no longer pink, turning once, about 8 minutes per side.
5. Put chops aside.

6. Add the cabbage and onion to the skillet and sauté until the vegetables have softened, for about 5 minutes.
7. Add the vinegar mixture and the apple slices to the skillet and bring the mixture to a boil.
8. Adjust heat to low and simmer, covered, for 5 additional minutes.
9. Return the pork chops to the skillet, along with any accumulated juices and thyme, cover, and cook for 5 more minutes.

Nutrition:

- Calories 223
- Carbohydrates 12 g.
- Fiber 3 g.

33. Chipotle Chili Pork Chops

Preparation time: 4 hours

Cooking time: 20 minutes

Servings: 4

Ingredients:

- Juice and zest of 1 lime
- 1 tbsp. extra-virgin olive oil
- 1 tbsp. chipotle chili powder
- 2 tsps. minced garlic
- 1 tsp. ground cinnamon
- Pinch sea salt
- 4 (5-oz.) pork chops
- Lime wedges

Directions:

1. Combine the lime juice and zest, oil, chipotle chili powder, garlic, cinnamon, and salt in a resealable plastic bag. Add the pork chops. Remove as much air as possible and seal the bag.
2. Marinate the chops in the refrigerator for at least 4 hours, and up to 24 hours, turning them several times.
3. Ready the oven to 400 °F and set a rack on a baking sheet. Let the chops rest at room temperature for 15 minutes, then arrange them on the rack and discard the remaining marinade.
4. Roast the chops until cooked through, turning once, about 10 minutes per side.
5. Serve with lime wedges.

Nutrition:

- Calories 204
- Carbohydrates 1 g.
- Sugar 1 g.

34. Orange-Marinated Pork Tenderloin

Preparation time: 2 hours

Cooking time: 30 minutes

Servings: 4

Ingredients:

- 1/4 c. freshly squeezed orange juice
- 2 tsps. orange zest
- 2 tsps. minced garlic
- 1 tsp. low-sodium soy sauce
- 1 tsp. grated fresh ginger
- 1 tsp. honey
- 1 1/2 lbs. pork tenderloin roast
- 1 tbsp. extra-virgin olive oil

Directions:

1. Blend together the orange juice, zest, garlic, soy sauce, ginger, and honey.
2. Pour the marinade into a resealable plastic bag and add the pork tenderloin.
3. Remove as much air as possible and seal the bag. Marinate the pork in the refrigerator, turning the bag a few times, for 2 hours.
4. Preheat the oven to 400 °F.
5. Pull out tenderloin from the marinade and discard the marinade.
6. Position big ovenproof skillet over medium-high heat and add the oil.
7. Sear the pork tenderloin on all sides, about 5 minutes in total.
8. Position skillet to the oven and roast for 25 minutes.
9. Put aside for 10 minutes before serving.

Nutrition:

- Calories 228
- Carbohydrates 4 g.
- Sugar 3 g.

35. Homestyle Herb Meatballs

Preparation time: 10 minutes   **Servings:** 4

Cooking time: 15 minutes

Ingredients:

- 1/2-lb. lean ground pork
- 1/2-lb. lean ground beef
- 1 sweet onion, finely chopped
- 1/4 c. bread crumbs

- 2 tbsps chopped fresh basil
- 2 tsps. minced garlic
- 1 egg
- Salt and pepper, to taste

Directions:

1. Preheat the oven to 350 °F.
2. Prepare a baking tray with parchment paper and set it aside.
3. In a large bowl, mix together the pork, beef, onion, bread crumbs, basil, garlic, egg, salt, and pepper until very well mixed.
4. Roll the meat mixture into 2-in. meatballs.
5. Transfer the meatballs to the baking sheet and bake until they are browned and cooked through, about 15 minutes.
6. Serve the meatballs with your favorite marinara sauce and some steamed green beans.

Nutrition:

- Calories 332

- Carbohydrates 13 g.
- Sugar 3 g.

36. Lime-Parsley Lamb Cutlets

Preparation time: 4 hours   **Servings:** 4

Cooking time: 10 minutes

Ingredients:

- 1/4 c. extra-virgin olive oil
- 1/4 c. freshly squeezed lime juice
- 2 tbsps lime zest

- 2 tbsps chopped fresh parsley
- 12 lamb cutlets (about 1 1/2 lbs. total)
- Salt and pepper, to taste

Directions:

1. Scourge the oil, lime juice, zest, parsley, salt, and pepper.
2. Pour the marinade into a resealable plastic bag.
3. Add the cutlets to the bag and remove as much air as possible before sealing.
4. Marinate the lamb in the refrigerator for about 4 hours, turning the bag several times.
5. Preheat the oven to broil.
6. Remove the chops from the bag and arrange them on an aluminum foil-lined baking sheet. Discard the marinade.
7. Broil the chops for 4 minutes per side for medium doneness.

8. Let the chops rest for 5 minutes before serving.

Nutrition:

- Calories 413
- Carbohydrates 1 g.
- Protein 31 g.

37. Mediterranean Steak Sandwiches

Preparation time: 1 hour

Cooking time: 10 minutes

Servings: 4

Ingredients:

- 2 tbsps extra-virgin olive oil
- 2 tbsps balsamic vinegar
- 2 tsps. garlic
- 2 tsps. lemon juice
- 2 tsps. fresh oregano
- 1 tsp. fresh parsley

- 1-pound flank steak
- 4 whole-wheat pitas
- 2 c. shredded lettuce
- 1 red onion, thinly sliced
- 1 tomato, chopped
- 1 oz. low-sodium feta cheese

Directions:

1. Scourge olive oil, balsamic vinegar, garlic, lemon juice, oregano, and parsley.
2. Add the steak to the bowl, turning to coat it completely.
3. Marinate the steak for 1 hour in the refrigerator, turning it over several times.
4. Preheat the broiler. Line a baking sheet with aluminum foil.
5. Put the steak out of the bowl and discard the marinade.
6. Situate the steak on the baking sheet and broil for 5 minutes per side for medium.
7. Set aside for 10 minutes before slicing.
8. Stuff the pitas with the sliced steak, lettuce, onion, tomato, and feta.

Nutrition:

- Calories 344
- Carbohydrates 22 g.
- Fiber 3 g.

Chapter 7. Salad

38. Thai Quinoa Salad

Preparation time: 10 minutes

Cooking time: 0 minutes

Servings: 1–2

Ingredients:

For the Dressing

- 1 tbsp. sesame seed
- 1 tsp. chopped garlic
- 1 tsp. lemon, fresh juice
- 3 tsp. apple cider vinegar
- 2 tsp. tamari, gluten-free.
- 1/4 c of tahini (sesame butter)
- 1 pitted date

- 1/2 tsp. salt
- 1/2 tsp. toasted sesame oil

For the Salad

- 1 c of quinoa, steamed
- 1 big handful of arugulas
- 1 tomato cut into pieces
- 1/4 of the red onion, diced

Directions:

1. Add filtered water and all the ingredients for the dressing into a small blender. Mix.
2. Steam the quinoa in a steamer or a rice pan, then set aside.
3. Combine the quinoa, the arugula, the tomatoes sliced, the red onion diced on a serving plate or bowl, add the Thai dressing and serve with a spoon.

Nutrition:

- Calories 100

- Carbohydrates 12 g.

39. Green Goddess Bowl and Avocado Cumin Dressing

Preparation time: 10 minutes

Cooking time: 0 minutes

Servings: 1–2

Ingredients:

For the Avocado Cumin Dressing

- 1 avocado
- 1 tbsp. cumin powder
- 2 limes, freshly squeezed
- 1 c of filtered water

- 1/4 seconds. sea salt
- 1 tbsp. olive extra-virgin olive oil
- Cayenne pepper dash
- Optional: 1/4 tsp. smoked pepper

For the Lemon Tahini Dressing

- 1/4 c of tahini (sesame butter)
- 1/2 c of filtered water (more if you want it thinner; less if you want it thicker)
- 1/2 lemon, freshly squeezed
- 1 clove of minced garlic
- 3/4 tsp. sea salt (Celtic Gray, Himalayan, Redmond Real Salt)
- 1 tbsp. olive extra-virgin olive oil
- Black pepper taste

For the Salad

- 3 c of kale, chopped
- 1/2 c of broccoli flowers, chopped
- 1/2 zucchini (make spiral noodles)
- 1/2 c of kelp noodles, soaked and drained
- 1/3 c of cherry tomatoes, halved.
- 2 tsp. hemp seeds

Directions:

1. Gently steam the kale and the broccoli (set the steam for 4 minutes), set aside.
2. Mix the zucchini noodles and kelp noodles and toss with a generous portion of the smoked avocado cumin dressing. Add the cherry tomatoes and stir again.
3. Place the steamed kale and broccoli and drizzle with the lemon tahini dressing. Top the kale and the broccoli with the noodles and tomatoes and sprinkle the whole dish with the hemp seeds.

Nutrition:

- Calories 89
- Carbohydrates 11 g.
- Fat 1.2 g.
- Protein 4 g.

40. 7 Sweet and Savory Salad

Preparation time: 10 minutes

Cooking time: 0 minutes

Servings: 1–2

Ingredients:

- 1 big head of butter lettuce
- 1/2 of cucumber, sliced
- 1 pomegranate, seed, or 1/3 c of seed
- 1 avocado, 1 cubed
- 1/4 c of shelled pistachio, chopped

For the Dressing

- 1/4 c of apple cider vinegar
- 1/2 c of olive oil
- 1 clove of garlic, minced

Directions:

1. Put the butter lettuce in a salad bowl.
2. Add the remaining ingredients and toss with the salad dressing.

Nutrition:

- Calories 68
- Carbohydrates 8 g.
- Fat 1.2 g.

- Protein 2 g.

41.   Kale Pesto's Pasta

Preparation time: 10 minutes

Servings: 1–2

Cooking time: 0 minutes

Ingredients:

- 1 bunch of kale
- 2 c of fresh basil
- 1/4 c of extra-virgin olive oil
- 1/2 c of walnuts
- 2 limes, freshly squeezed
- .

- Sea salt and chili pepper
- 1 zucchini, noodle (spiralizer)
- Optional: garnish with chopped asparagus, spinach leaves, and tomato

Directions:

1. The night before, soak the walnuts in order to improve absorption.
2. Put all the kale pesto ingredients in a blender and blend until the consistency of the cream is reached.
3. Add the zucchini noodles and enjoy.

Nutrition:

- Calories 55

- Carbohydrates 9 g
- Fat 1.2 g.

42.   Beet Salad with Basil Dressing

Preparation time: 10 minutes

Servings: 4

Cooking time: 0 minutes

Ingredients:

For the Dressing

- 1/4 c. blackberries
- 1/4 c. extra-virgin olive oil
- Juice of 1 lemon
- 2 tbsps minced fresh basil
- 1 tsp. poppy seeds

- A pinch of sea salt

For the Salad

- 2 celery stalks, chopped
- 4 cooked beets, peeled and chopped
- 1 c. blackberries
- 4 c. spring mix

Directions:

1. To make the dressing, mash the blackberries in a bowl. Whisk in the oil, lemon juice, basil, poppy seeds, and sea salt.
2. To make the salad: Add the celery, beets, blackberries, and spring mix to the bowl with the dressing.
3. Combine and serve.

Nutrition:

- Calories 192
- Fat 15 g.
- Carbohydrates 15 g.

- Protein 2 g.

43. Basic Salad with Olive Oil Dressing

Preparation time: 10 minutes

Servings: 4

Cooking time: 0 minute

Ingredients:

- 1 c. coarsely chopped iceberg lettuce
- 1 c. coarsely chopped romaine lettuce
- 1 c. fresh baby spinach

- 1 large tomato, hulled and coarsely chopped
- 1 c. diced cucumber
- 2 tbsps extra-virgin olive oil
- 1/4 tsp of sea salt

Directions:

1. In a bowl, combine the spinach and lettuces. Add the tomato and cucumber.
2. Drizzle with oil and sprinkle with sea salt.
3. Mix and serve.

Nutrition:

- Calories 77
- Fat 4 g.

- Carbohydrates 3 g.
- Protein 1 g.

44. Spinach and Orange Salad with Oil Drizzle

Preparation time: 10 minutes

Servings: 4

Cooking time: 0 minute

Ingredients:

- 4 c. fresh baby spinach
- 1 blood orange, coarsely chopped
- 1/2 red onion, thinly sliced
- 1/2 shallot, finely chopped

- 2 tbsp. minced fennel fronds
- Juice of 1 lemon
- 1 tbsp. extra-virgin olive oil
- Pinch sea salt

Directions:

1. In a bowl, toss together the spinach, orange, red onion, shallot, and fennel fronds.
2. Add the lemon juice, oil, and sea salt.
3. Mix and serve.

Nutrition:

- Calories 79
- Fat 2 g.

- Carbohydrates 8 g.
- Protein 1 g.

45. Fruit Salad with Coconut-Lime Dressing

Preparation time: 5 minutes

Cooking time: 0 minutes

Servings: 4

Ingredients:

For the Dressing

- 1/4 c. full-fat canned coconut milk
- 1 tbsp. raw honey
- Juice of 1/2 lime
- Pinch sea salt

- For the salad
- 2 bananas, thinly sliced
- 2 mandarin oranges, segmented
- 1/2 c. strawberries, thinly sliced
- 1/2 c. raspberries
- 1/2 c. blueberries

Directions:

1. To make the dressing: Whisk all the dressing ingredients in a bowl.
2. To make the salad: Add the salad ingredients to a bowl and mix.
3. Drizzle with the dressing and serve.

Nutrition:

- Calories 141
- Fat 3 g.

- Carbohydrates 30 g.
- Protein 2 g.

46. Cranberry and Brussels Sprouts with Dressing

Preparation time: 10 minutes

Servings: 4

Cooking time: 0 minute

Ingredients:

For the Dressing

- 1/3 c. extra-virgin olive oil
- 2 tbsp. apple cider vinegar
- 1 tbsp. pure maple syrup
- Juice of 1 orange
- 1/2 tbsp. dried rosemary
- 1 tbsp. scallion, whites only

- Pinch sea salt

For the Salad

- 1 bunch scallions, greens only, finely chopped
- 1 c. Brussels sprouts, stemmed, halved, and thinly sliced
- 1/2 c. fresh cranberries
- 4 c. fresh baby spinach

Directions:

1. To make the dressing: In a bowl, whisk the dressing ingredients.
2. To make the salad: Add the scallions, Brussels sprouts, cranberries, and spinach to the bowl with the dressing.
3. Combine and serve.

Nutrition:

- Calories 267
- Fat 18 g.
- Carbohydrates 26 g.
- Protein 2 g.

47. Parsnip, Carrot, and Kale Salad with Dressing

Preparation time: 10 minutes

Servings: 4

Cooking time: 0 minutes

Ingredients:

For the Dressing

- 1/3 c. extra-virgin olive oil
- Juice of 1 lime
- 2 tbsp. minced fresh mint leaves
- 1 tsp. pure maple syrup
- Pinch sea salt

For the Salad

- 1 bunch kale, chopped
- 1/2 parsnip, grated
- 1/2 carrot, grated
- 2 tbsp. sesame seeds

Directions:

1. To make the dressing, mix all the dressing ingredients in a bowl.
2. To make the salad, add the kale to the dressing and massage the dressing into the kale for 1 minute.
3. Add the parsnip, carrot, and sesame seeds.
4. Combine and serve.

Nutrition:

- Calories 214
- Fat 2 g.
- Carbohydrates 12 g.
- Protein 2 g.

48. Tomato Toasts

Preparation time: 5 minutes

Servings: 4

Cooking time: 5 minutes

Ingredients:

- 4 slices of sprouted bread toasts
- 2 tomatoes, sliced
- 1 avocado, mashed
- 1 tsp. olive oil
- 1 pinch of salt
- 3/4 teaspoon ground black pepper

Directions:

1. Blend together the olive oil, mashed avocado, salt, and ground black pepper.
2. When the mixture is homogenous, spread it over the sprouted bread.
3. Then place the sliced tomatoes over the toasts.
4. Enjoy!

Nutrition:

- Calories 125

- Fat 11.1 g.
- Carbohydrates 7.0 g.
- Protein 1.5 g.

49. Every Day Salad

Preparation time: 10 minutes

Cooking time: 40 minutes

Servings: 6

Ingredients:

- 5 halved mushrooms
- 6 halved cherry (plum) tomatoes
- 6 rinsed lettuce leaves
- 10 olives
- 1/2 chopped cucumber
- Juice from 1/2 key lime
- 1 tsp. olive oil
- Pure sea salt

Directions:

1. Tear rinsed lettuce leaves into medium pieces and put them in a medium salad bowl.
2. Add mushrooms halves, chopped cucumber, olives, and cherry tomato halves into the bowl. Mix well. Pour olive and key lime juice over the salad.
3. Add pure sea salt to taste. Mix it all till it is well combined.

Nutrition:

- Calories 88
- Carbohydrates 11 g.
- Fat: .5 g.
- Protein: .8 g.

Chapter 9. Appetizer Recipes

50. Aromatic Toasted Pumpkin Seeds

Preparation time: 5 minutes   **Servings:** 4

Cooking time: 45 minutes

Ingredients:
- 2 packets stevia
- 1 tbsp. canola oil
- 1/4 tsp. sea salt
- 1 c. pumpkin seeds
- 1 tsp. cinnamon

Directions:

1. Prep the oven to 300 °F (150°C).
2. Combine the pumpkin seeds with cinnamon, stevia, canola oil, and salt in a bowl. Stir to mix well.
3. Pour the seeds in a single layer on a baking sheet, then arrange the sheet in the preheated oven.
4. Bake for 45 minutes or until well toasted and fragrant. Shake the sheet twice to bake the seeds evenly.
5. Serve immediately.

Nutrition:
- Carbohydrates 5.1 g.
- Fiber 2.3 g.
- Calories 202

51. Bacon-Wrapped Shrimps

Preparation time: 10 minutes   **Servings:** 10

Cooking time: 6 minutes

Ingredients:
- 7 slices bacon
- 4 leaves romaine lettuce
- 20 shrimps, peeled and deveined

Directions:

1. Set the oven to 205 °C.
2. Wrap each shrimp with each bacon strip, then arrange the wrapped shrimps in a single layer on a baking sheet, seam side down.
3. Broil for 6 minutes. Flip the shrimps halfway through the cooking time.
4. Take out from the oven and serve on lettuce leaves.

Nutrition:
- Calories 70
- Fat 4.5 g.

- Protein 7 g.

52. Cheesy Broccoli Bites

Preparation time: 10 minutes   **Servings:** 6

Cooking time: 25 minutes

Ingredients:

- 2 tbsps olive oil
- 2 heads broccoli, trimmed
- 1 egg
- 1/3 c. reduced-fat shredded Cheddar cheese

- 1 egg white
- 1/2 c. onion, chopped
- 1/3 c. bread crumbs
- 1/4 tsp. salt
- 1/4 tsp. black pepper

Directions:

1. Ready the oven at 400 °F (205 °C). Coat a large baking sheet with olive oil.
2. Arrange a colander in a saucepan, then place the broccoli in the colander. Pour the water into the saucepan to cover the bottom. Boil, then reduce the heat to low. Close and simmer for 6 minutes. Allow cooling for 10 minutes.
3. Blend the broccoli and the remaining ingredients in a food processor. Let sit for 10 minutes.
4. Make the bites: Drop 1 tbsp of the mixture on the baking sheet. Repeat with the remaining mixture.
5. Bake in the preheated oven for 25 minutes. Flip the bites halfway through the cooking time.
6. Serve immediately.

Nutrition:

- Calories 100

- Carbohydrates 13 g.
- Fiber 3 g.

53. Easy Caprese Skewers

Preparation time: 5 minutes

Cooking time: 0 minute

Servings: 2

Ingredients:

- 12 cherry tomatoes
- 8 (1-in.) pieces Mozzarella cheese

- 12 basil leaves
- 1/4 c. Italian Vinaigrette, for serving

Directions:

1. Thread the tomatoes, cheese, and bay leaf alternatively through the skewers.
2. Place the skewers on a big plate and baste with the Italian vinaigrette. Serve immediately.

Nutrition:

- Calories 230

- Carbohydrates 8.5 g.
- Fiber 1.9 g.

54.   Grilled Tofu with Sesame Seeds

Preparation time: 45 minutes

Servings: 6

Cooking time: 20 minutes

Ingredients:

- 1 1/2 tbsps brown rice vinegar
- 1 scallion
- 1 tbsp. ginger root
- 1 tbsp. no-sugar-added applesauce
- 2 tbsps naturally brewed soy sauce
- 1/4 tsp. dried red pepper flakes

- 2 tsps. sesame oil, toasted
- 1 (14-oz./397 g.) package extra-firm tofu
- 2 tbsps fresh cilantro
- 1 tsp. sesame seeds

Directions:

1. Combine the vinegar, scallion, ginger, applesauce, soy sauce, red pepper flakes, and sesame oil in a large bowl. Stir to mix well.
2. Dunk the tofu pieces in the bowl, then refrigerate to marinate for 30 minutes.
3. Preheat a grill pan over medium-high heat.
4. Place the tofu on the grill pan with tongs, reserve the marinade, then grill for 8 minutes or until the tofu is golden brown and have deep grilled marks on both sides. Flip the tofu halfway through the cooking time. You may need to work in batches to avoid overcrowding.
5. Transfer the tofu to a large plate and sprinkle with cilantro leaves and sesame seeds. Serve with the marinade alongside.

Nutrition:

- Calories 90

- Carbohydrates 3 g.
- Fiber 1 g.

55.   Kale Chips

Preparation time: 5 minutes

Servings: 1

Cooking time: 15 minutes

Ingredients:

- 1/4 tsp. garlic powder
- Pinch cayenne to taste

- 1 tbsp. extra-virgin olive oil
- 1/2 teaspoon sea salt, or to taste
- 1 (8-oz.) bunch kale

Directions:

1. Prepare the oven at 180 °C. Line 2 baking sheets with parchment paper.
2. Toss the garlic powder, cayenne pepper, olive oil, and salt in a large bowl, then dunk the kale in the bowl.

3. Situate the kale in a single layer on one of the baking sheets.
4. Arrange the sheet in the preheated oven and bake for 7 minutes. Remove the sheet from the oven and pour the kale into the single layer of the other baking sheet.
5. Move the sheet of kale back to the oven and bake for another 7 minutes.
6. Serve immediately.

Nutrition:

- Calories 136

- Carbohydrates 3 g.
- Fiber 1.1 g.

56. Simple Deviled Eggs

Preparation time: 5 minutes

Servings: 12

Cooking time: 8 minutes

Ingredients:

- 6 large eggs
- 1/8 tsp. mustard powder

- 2 tbsps light mayonnaise
- Salt and pepper, to taste

Directions:

1. Sit the eggs in a saucepan, then pour in enough water to cover the egg. Bring to a boil, then boil the eggs for another 8 minutes. Turn off the heat and cover, then let sit for 15 minutes.
2. Transfer the boiled eggs to a pot of cold water and peel under the water.
3. Transfer the eggs to a large plate, then cut in half. Remove the egg yolks and place them in a bowl, then mash with a fork.
4. Add the mustard powder, mayo, salt, and pepper to the bowl of yolks, then stir to mix well.
5. Spoon the yolk mixture in the egg white on the plate. Serve immediately.

Nutrition:

- Calories 45

- Carbohydrates 1 g.
- Fiber 0.9 g.

57. Sautéed Collard Greens and Cabbage

Preparation time: 10 minutes

Servings: 8

Cooking time: 10 minutes

Ingredients:

- 2 tbsps extra-virgin olive oil
- 1 collard greens bunch

- 1/2 small green cabbage
- 6 garlic cloves
- 1 tbsp. low-sodium soy sauce

Directions:

1. Cook olive oil in a large skillet over medium-high heat.
2. Sauté the collard greens in the oil for about 2 minutes, or until the greens start to wilt.

3. Toss in the cabbage and mix well. Set to medium-low, cover, and cook for 5–7 minutes, stirring occasionally, or until the greens are softened.
4. Fold in the garlic and soy sauce and stir to combine. Cook for about 30 seconds more until fragrant.
5. Remove from the heat to a plate and serve.

Nutrition:

- Calories 73
- Carbohydrates 5.9 g.
- Fiber 2.9 g.

58. Roasted Delicata Squash with Thyme

Preparation time: 10 minutes

Servings: 4

Cooking time: 20 minutes

Ingredients:

- 1 (1 1/2-pound) Delicata squash
- 1 tbsp. extra-virgin olive oil
- 1/2 teaspoon dried thyme
- 1/4 tsp. salt
- 1/4 tsp. freshly ground black pepper

Directions:

1. Prep the oven to 400 °F (205 °C). Prepare a baking sheet with parchment paper and set it aside.
2. Add the squash strips, olive oil, thyme, salt, and pepper in a large bowl, and toss until the squash strips are fully coated.
3. Place the squash strips on the prepared baking sheet in a single layer. Roast for about 20 minutes, flipping the strips halfway through.
4. Remove from the oven and serve on plates.

Nutrition:

- Calories 78
- Carbohydrates 11.8 g.
- Fiber 2.1 g.

59. Roasted Asparagus and Red Peppers

Preparation time: 5 minutes

Servings: 4

Cooking time: 15 minutes

Ingredients:

- 1-pound (454 g) asparagus
- 2 red bell peppers, seeded
- 1 small onion
- 2 tbsps Italian dressing

Directions:

1. Ready oven to (205 °C). Wrap a baking sheet with parchment paper and set it aside.
2. Combine the asparagus with the peppers, onion, dressing in a large bowl, and toss well.

3. Arrange the vegetables on the baking sheet and roast for about 15 minutes. Flip the vegetables with a spatula once during cooking.
4. Transfer to a large platter and serve.

Nutrition:

- Calories 92
- Carbohydrates 10.7 g.
- Fiber 4 g.

60. Tarragon Spring Peas

Preparation time: 10 minutes

Servings: 6

Cooking time: 12 minutes

Ingredients:

- 1 tbsp. unsalted butter
- 1/2 Vidalia onion
-
- 1 c. low-sodium vegetable broth
- 3 c. fresh shelled peas
- 1 tbsp. minced fresh tarragon

Directions:

1. Cook butter in a pan at medium heat.
2. Sauté the onion in the melted butter for about 3 minutes, stirring occasionally.
3. Pour in the vegetable broth and whisk well. Add the peas and tarragon to the skillet and stir to combine.
4. Reduce the heat to low, cover, cook for about 8 minutes more, or until the peas are tender.
5. Let the peas cool for 5 minutes and serve warm.

Nutrition:

- Calories 82
- Carbohydrates 12 g.
- Fiber 3.8 g.

61. Butter-Orange Yams

Preparation time: 7 minutes

Cooking time: 45 minutes

Servings: 8

Ingredients:

- 2 medium jewel yams
- 2 tbsps unsalted butter
- Juice of 1 large orange
- 1 1/2 tsps. ground cinnamon
- 1/4 tsp. ground ginger

- 3/4 teaspoon ground nutmeg
- 1/8 tsp. ground cloves

Directions:

1. Set oven at 180 °C.
2. Arrange the yam dices on a rimmed baking sheet in a single layer. Set aside.
3. Add the butter, orange juice, cinnamon, ginger, nutmeg, and garlic cloves to a medium saucepan over medium-low heat. Cook for 3–5 minutes, stirring continuously.
4. Spoon the sauce over the yams and toss to coat well.
5. Bake in the prepared oven for 40 minutes.
6. Let the yams cool for 8 minutes on the baking sheet before removing and serving.

Nutrition:

- Calories 129
- Carbohydrates 24.7 g.
- Fiber 5 g.

Chapter 11. Meat Recipes

62. Pork Chops with Grape Sauce

Preparation time: 15 minutes

Servings: 4

Cooking time: 25 minutes

Ingredients:

- Cooking spray
- 4 pork chops
- 1/4 c. onion, sliced
- 1 clove garlic, minced
- 1/2 c. low-sodium chicken broth

- 3/4 c. apple juice
- 1 tbsp. cornstarch
- 1 tbsp. balsamic vinegar
- 1 tsp. honey
- 1 c. seedless red grapes, sliced in half

Directions:

1. Spray oil on your pan.
2. Put it over medium heat.
3. Add the pork chops to the pan.
4. Cook for 5 minutes per side.
5. Remove and set aside.
6. Add the onion and garlic.
7. Cook for 2 minutes.
8. Pour in the broth and apple juice.
9. Bring to a boil.

10. Reduce the heat to simmer.
11. Put the pork chops back to the skillet.
12. Simmer for 4 minutes.
13. In a bowl, mix the cornstarch, vinegar, and honey.
14. Add to the pan.
15. Cook until the sauce has thickened.
16. Add the grapes.
17. Pour the sauce over the pork chops before serving.

Nutrition:

- Calories 188
- Total Fat 4 g.
- Saturated Fat 1 g.
- Cholesterol 47 mg
- Sodium 117 mg

- Total Carbohydrate 18 g.
- Dietary Fiber 1 g.
- Total Sugars 13 g.
- Protein 19 g.
- Potassium 759 mg.

63. Roasted Pork and Apples

Preparation time: 15 minutes

Servings: 4

Cooking time: 30 minutes

Ingredients:

- Salt and pepper to taste
- 1 lb. pork tenderloin
- 1 tbsp. canola oil

- 1 onion, sliced into wedges
- 3 cooking apples, sliced into wedges
- 2/3 c. apple cider
- Sprigs fresh sage

Directions:

1. In a bowl, mix salt, pepper, and sage.
2. Season both sides of pork with this mixture.
3. Place a pan over medium heat.
4. Brown both sides.
5. Transfer to a roasting pan.
6. Add the onion on top and around the pork.
7. Drizzle oil on top of the pork and apples.
8. Roast in the oven at 425 °F for 10 minutes.
9. Add the apples, roast for another 15 minutes.
10. In a pan, boil the apple cider and then simmer for 10 minutes.
11. Pour the apple cider sauce over the pork before serving.

Nutrition:

- Calories 239
- Total Fat 6 g.
- Saturated Fat 1 g.
- Cholesterol 74 mg
- Sodium 209 mg

- Total Carbohydrate 22 g.
- Dietary Fiber 3 g.
- Total Sugars 16 g.
- Protein 24 g.
- Potassium 655 mg.

64.   Pork with Cranberry Relish

Preparation time: 30 minutes

Cooking time: 30 minutes

Servings: 4

Ingredients:

- 12 oz. pork tenderloin, fat trimmed and sliced crosswise
- Salt and pepper to taste
- 1/4 c. all-purpose flour

- 2 tbsps olive oil
- 1 onion, sliced thinly
- 1/4 c. dried cranberries
- 1/4 c. low-sodium chicken broth
- 1 tbsp. balsamic vinegar

Directions:

1. Flatten each slice of the pork using a mallet.
2. In a dish, mix the salt, pepper, and flour.
3. Dip each pork slice into the flour mixture.
4. Add oil to a pan over medium-high heat.
5. Cook the pork for 3 minutes per side or until golden crispy.
6. Transfer to a serving plate and cover with foil.
7. Cook the onion in the pan for 4 minutes.
8. Stir in the rest of the ingredients.
9. Simmer until the sauce has thickened.

Nutrition:

- Calories 211

- Total Fat 9 g.
- Saturated Fat 2 g.
- Cholesterol 53 mg

- Sodium 116 mg
- Total Carbohydrate 15 g.
- Dietary Fiber 1 g.
- Total Sugars 6 g.

- Protein 18 g.
- Potassium 378 mg.

65.   Sesame Pork with Mustard Sauce

Preparation time: 25 minutes

Cooking time: 25 minutes

Servings: 4

Ingredients:

- 2 tbsps low-sodium teriyaki sauce
- 1/4 c. chili sauce
- 2 cloves garlic, minced
- 2 tsps. ginger, grated
- 2 pork tenderloins

- 2 tsps. sesame seeds
- 1/4 c. low-fat sour cream
- 1 tsp. Dijon mustard
- Salt to taste
- 1 scallion, chopped

Directions:

1. Preheat your oven to 425 °F.
2. Mix the teriyaki sauce, chili sauce, garlic, and ginger.
3. Put the pork on a roasting pan.
4. Brush the sauce on both sides of the pork.
5. Bake in the oven for 15 minutes.
6. Brush with more sauce.
7. Top with sesame seeds.
8. Roast for 10 more minutes.
9. Mix the rest of the ingredients.
10. Serve the pork with mustard sauce.

Nutrition:

- Calories 135
- Total Fat 3 g.
- Saturated Fat 1 g.
- Cholesterol 56X mg
- Sodium 302 mg

- Total Carbohydrate 7 g
- Dietary Fiber 1 g.
- Total Sugars 15 g.
- Protein 20 g.
- Potassium 755 mg.

66.   Steak with Mushroom Sauce

Preparation time: 20 minutes

Servings: 4

Cooking time: 5 minutes

Ingredients:

- 12 oz. sirloin steak, sliced and trimmed
- 2 tsps. grilling seasoning

- 2 tsps. oil
- 6 oz. broccoli, trimmed
- 2 c. frozen peas
- 3 c. fresh mushrooms, sliced
- 1 c. beef broth (unsalted)
- 1 tbsp. mustard
- 2 tsps. cornstarch
- Salt to taste

Directions:

1. Preheat your oven to 350 °F.
2. Season the meat with the grilling seasoning.
3. In a pan over medium-high heat, cook the meat and broccoli for 4 minutes.
4. Sprinkle the peas around the steak.
5. Put the pan inside the oven and bake for 8 minutes.
6. Remove both the meat and vegetables from the pan.
7. Add the mushrooms to the pan.
8. Cook for 3 minutes.
9. Mix the broth, mustard, salt and cornstarch.
10. Add to the mushrooms.
11. Cook for 1 minute.
12. Pour sauce over meat and vegetables before serving.

Nutrition:

- Calories 226
- Total Fat 6 g.
- Saturated Fat 2 g.
- Cholesterol 51 mg
- Sodium 356 mg
- Total Carbohydrate 16 g.
- Dietary Fiber 5 g.
- Total Sugars 6 g.
- Protein 26 g.
- Potassium 780 mg.

67.   Steak with Tomato and Herbs

Preparation time: 30 minutes

Servings: 2

Cooking time: 30 minutes

Ingredients:

- 8 oz. beef loin steak, sliced in half
- Salt and pepper to taste
- Cooking spray
- 1 tsp. fresh basil, snipped
- 1/4 c. green onion, sliced
- 1/2 c. tomato, chopped

Directions:

1. Season the steak with salt and pepper.
2. Spray oil on your pan.
3. Put the pan over medium-high heat.
4. Once hot, add the steaks.

5. Reduce the heat to medium.
6. Cook for 10–13 minutes for medium, turning once.
7. Add the basil and green onion.
8. Cook for 2 minutes.
9. Add the tomato.
10. Cook for 1 minute.
11. Let cool a little before slicing.

Nutrition:

- Calories 170
- Total Fat 6 g.
- Saturated Fat 2 g.
- Cholesterol 66 mg
- Sodium 207 mg

- Total Carbohydrate 3 g.
- Dietary Fiber 1 g.
- Total Sugars 5 g.
- Protein 25 g.
- Potassium 477 mg.

68. Barbecue Beef Brisket

Preparation time: 25 minutes

Servings: 10

Cooking time: 10 hours

Ingredients:

- 4 lb. beef brisket (boneless), trimmed and sliced
- 1 bay leaf
- 2 onions, sliced into rings
- 1/2 tsp. dried thyme, crushed

- 1/4 c. chili sauce
- 1 garlic clove, minced
- Salt and pepper to taste
- 2 tbsps light brown sugar
- 2 tbsps cornstarch
- 2 tbsps cold water

Directions:

1. Put the meat in a slow cooker.
2. Add the bay leaf and onion.
3. In a bowl, mix the thyme, chili sauce, salt, pepper, and sugar.
4. Pour the sauce over the meat.
5. Mix well.
6. Seal the pot and cook on low heat for 10 hours.
7. Discard the bay leaf.
8. Pour the cooking liquid into a pan.
9. Add the mixed water and cornstarch.
10. Simmer until the sauce has thickened.
11. Pour the sauce over the meat.

Nutrition:

- Calories 182
- Total Fat 6 g.
- Saturated Fat 2 g.
- Cholesterol 57 mg.

- Sodium 217 mg
- Total Sugars 4 g.
- Protein 20 g.
- Potassium 383 mg.

69. Beef and Asparagus

Preparation time: 15 minutes

Cooking time: 10 minutes

Servings: 4

Ingredients:

- 2 tsps. olive oil
- 1 lb. lean beef sirloin, trimmed and sliced
- 1 carrot, shredded
- Salt and pepper to taste
- 12 oz. asparagus, trimmed and sliced
- 1 tsp. dried herbes de Provence, crushed
- 1/2 c. Marsala
- 1/4 tsp. lemon zest

Directions:

1. Pour oil in a pan over medium heat.
2. Add the beef and carrot.
3. Season with salt and pepper.
4. Cook for 3 minutes.
5. Add the asparagus and herbs.
6. Cook for 2 minutes.
7. Add the Marsala and lemon zest.
8. Cook for 5 minutes, stirring frequently.

Nutrition:

- Calories 327
- Total Fat 7 g.
- Saturated Fat 2 g.
- Cholesterol 69 mg
- Sodium 209 mg
- Total Carbohydrate 29 g.
- Dietary Fiber 2 g.
- Total Sugars 3 g.
- Protein 28 g.
- Potassium 576 mg.

70. Italian Beef

Preparation time: 20 minutes

Cooking time: 1 hour and 20 minutes

Servings: 4

Ingredients:

- Cooking spray
- 1 lb. beef round steak, trimmed and sliced
- 1 c. onion, chopped
- 2 cloves garlic, minced
- 1 c. green bell pepper, chopped
- 1/2 c. celery, chopped
- 2 c. mushrooms, sliced
- 14 1/2 oz. canned diced tomatoes
- 1/2 tsp. dried basil
- 1/4 tsp. dried oregano
- 1/8 tsp. crushed red pepper
- 2 tbsps Parmesan cheese, grated

Directions:

1. Spray oil on the pan over medium heat.
2. Cook the meat until brown on both sides.
3. Transfer the meat to a plate.
4. Add the onion, garlic, bell pepper, celery, and mushroom to the pan.
5. Cook until tender.
6. Add the tomatoes, herbs, and pepper.
7. Put the meat back to the pan.
8. Simmer while covered for 1 hour and 15 minutes.
9. Stir occasionally.
10. Sprinkle Parmesan cheese on top of the dish before serving.

Nutrition:

- Calories 212
- Total Fat 4 g.
- Saturated Fat 1 g.
- Cholesterol 51 mg

- Sodium 296 mg
- Total Sugars 6 g.
- Protein 30 g.
- Potassium 876 mg.

71.   Lamb with Broccoli and Carrots

Preparation time: 20 minutes

Servings: 4

Cooking time: 10 minutes

Ingredients:

- 2 cloves garlic, minced
- 1 tbsp. fresh ginger, grated
- 1/4 tsp. red pepper, crushed
- 2 tbsps low-sodium soy sauce
- 1 tbsp. white vinegar
- 1 tbsp. cornstarch

- 12 oz. lamb meat, trimmed and sliced
- 2 tsps. cooking oil
- 1 lb. broccoli, sliced into florets
- 2 carrots, sliced into strips
- 3/4 c. low-sodium beef broth
- 4 green onions, chopped
- 2 c. cooked spaghetti squash pasta

Directions:

1. Combine the garlic, ginger, red pepper, soy sauce, vinegar, and cornstarch in a bowl.
2. Add the lamb to the marinade.
3. Marinate for 10 minutes.
4. Discard the marinade.
5. In a pan over medium heat, add the oil.
6. Add the lamb and cook for 3 minutes.
7. Transfer the lamb to a plate.
8. Add the broccoli and carrots.
9. Cook for 1 minute.
10. Pour in the beef broth.
11. Cook for 5 minutes.
12. Put the meat back to the pan.

13. Sprinkle with green onion and serve on top of spaghetti squash.

Nutrition:

- Calories 205
- Total Fat 6 g.
- Saturated Fat 1 g.

- Cholesterol 40 mg
- Sodium 659 mg
- Total Carbohydrate 17 g.

72.   Rosemary Lamb

Preparation time: 15 minutes

Servings: 14

Cooking time: 2 hours

Ingredients:

- Salt and pepper to taste
- 2 tsps. fresh rosemary, snipped

- 5 lb. whole leg of lamb, trimmed and cut with slits on all sides
- 3 cloves garlic, slivered
- 1 c. water

Directions:

1. Preheat your oven to 375 °F.
2. Mix salt, pepper, and rosemary in a bowl.
3. Sprinkle the mixture all over the lamb.
4. Insert slivers of garlic into the slits.
5. Put the lamb on a roasting pan.
6. Add water to the pan.
7. Roast for 2 hours.

Nutrition:

- Calories 136
- Total Fat 4 g.
- Saturated Fat 1 g.

- Cholesterol 71 mg
- Sodium 218 mg
- Protein 23 g.
- Potassium 248 mg

73.   Mediterranean Lamb Meatballs

Preparation time: 10 minutes

Servings: 8

Cooking time: 20 minutes

Ingredients:

- 12 oz. roasted red peppers
- 1 1/2 c. whole wheat breadcrumbs
- 2 eggs, beaten
- 1/3 c. tomato sauce

- 1/2 c. fresh basil
- 1/4 c. parsley, snipped
- Salt and pepper to taste
- 2 lb. lean ground lamb

Directions:

1. Preheat your oven to 350 °F.
2. In a bowl, mix all the ingredients and then form them into meatballs.
3. Put the meatballs on a baking pan.
4. Bake in the oven for 20 minutes.

Nutrition:

- Calories 94
- Total Fat 3 g.
- Saturated Fat 1 g.
- Cholesterol 35 mg
- Sodium 170 mg
- Total Carbohydrate 2 g.
- Dietary Fiber 1 g.
- Total Sugars 0 g.

Chapter 14. Snacks and Bread

74. Chick Pea and Kale Dish

Preparation time: 10 minutes

Servings: 4

Cooking time: 25 30 minutes

Ingredients:

- 2 c. chickpea flour
- 1/2 c. green bell pepper, diced
- 1/2 c. onions, minced
- 1 tbsp. oregano

- 1 tbsp. salt
- 1 tsp. cayenne
- 4 c. spring water
- 2 tbsps grape seed oil

Directions:

1. Boil spring water in a large pot.
2. Lower heat into medium and whisk in chickpea flour.
3. Add some minced onions, diced green bell pepper, and seasoning to the pot, and cook for 10 minutes.
4. Cover the dish using a baking sheet, grease with oil.
5. Pour the batter into the sheet and spread with a spatula.
6. Cover with another sheet.
7. Transfer to a fridge and chill for 20 minutes.
8. Remove from the freezer and cut the batter into fry shapes.
9. Preheat the air fryer, to 385 °F.
10. Transfer the fries into the cooking basket, lightly greased, and cover with parchment
11. Bake for about 15 minutes; flip and bake for 10 minutes more until golden brown
12. Serve and enjoy!

Nutrition:

- Calories 271
- Carbohydrates 28 g.

- Fat 15 g.
- Protein 9 g.

75. Zucchini Chips

Preparation time: 10 minutes

Servings: 4

Cooking time: 12–15 minutes

Ingredients:

- Salt as needed

- Grapeseed oil as needed
- 6 zucchinis

Directions:

1. Preheat the air fryer at 330 °F,
2. Wash zucchini and slice it into thin strips.
3. Put slices in a bowl and add oil, salt, and toss.
4. Spread over the cooking basket, fry for 12–15 minutes.
5. Serve and enjoy!

Nutrition:

- Calories 92
- Carbohydrates 6 g.
- Fat 7 g.
- Protein 2 g.

76. Classic Blueberry Spelt Muffins

Preparation time: 10 minutes

Servings: 4

Cooking time: 12–15 minutes

Ingredients:

- 1/4 sea salt
- 1/3 c. maple syrup
- 1 tsp. baking powder
- 1/2 c. sea moss
- 3/4 c. spelt flour
- 3/4 c. Kamut flour
- 1 c. hemp milk
- 1 c. blueberries

Directions:

1. Preheat the air fryer at 380 °F.
2. Take your muffin tins and gently grease them.
3. Take a bowl and add flour, syrup, salt, baking powder, sea moss and mix well.
4. Add milk and mix well.
5. Fold in blueberries.
6. Pour into muffin tins.
7. Transfer to the cooking basket and bake for 20–25 minutes until nicely baked.
8. Serve and enjoy!

Nutrition:

- Calories 217
- Carbohydrates 32 g.
- Fat 9 g.
- Protein 4 g.

77. Genuine Healthy Crackers

Preparation time: 10 minutes

Servings: 4

Cooking time: 12–15 minutes

Ingredients:

- 1/2 c. Rye flour
- 1 c. spelt flour
- 2 tsps. sesame seed
- 1 tsp. agave syrup

- 1 tsp. salt
- 2 tbsps grapeseed oil
- 3/4 c. spring water

Directions:

1. Preheat the air fryer at 330 °F.
2. Take a medium bowl and add all the ingredients; mix well.
3. Make a dough ball.
4. Prepare a place for rolling out the dough, cover with a piece of parchment.
5. Lightly grease a paper with grape seed oil and place the dough.
6. Roll out the dough with a rolling pin; add more flour if needed.
7. Take a shape cutter and cut the dough into squares.
8. Place the squares in the air fryer cooking basket.
9. Brush with more oil.
10. Sprinkle salt.
11. Bake for 10–15 minutes until golden.
12. Let it cool, serve, and enjoy!

Nutrition:

- Calories 226
- Carbohydrates 41 g.
- Fat 3 g.
- Protein 11 g.

78. Tortilla Chips

Preparation time: 10 minutes

Servings: 4

Cooking time: 8–12 minutes

Ingredients:

- 2 c of spelt flour
- 1 tsp of salt
- 1/2 c of spring water
- 1/3 c of grapeseed oil

Directions:

1. Preheat your air fryer to 320 °F.
2. Take the food processor then add salt, flour, and process well for 15 seconds.
3. Gradually add grapeseed oil until mixed.
4. Keep mixing until you have a nice dough.
5. Prepare a work surface and cover with a piece of parchment; sprinkle flour.
6. Knead the dough for 1–2 minutes.
7. Grease a cooking basket with oil.
8. Transfer the dough to the cooking basket, brush oil and sprinkle salt.
9. Cut the dough into 8 triangles.
10. Bake for about 8–12 minutes until golden brown.
11. Serve and enjoy once done!

Nutrition:

- Calories 288
- Carbohydrates 18 g.
- Fat 17 g.
- Protein 16 g.

79.   Pumpkin Spice Crackers

Preparation time: 10 minutes

Servings: 06

Cooking time: 60 minutes

Ingredients:

- 1/3 c. coconut flour
- 2 tbsps pumpkin pie spice
- 3/4 c. sunflower seeds
- 3/4 c. flaxseed
- 1/3 c. sesame seeds
- 1 tbsp. ground psyllium husk powder
- 1 tsp. sea salt
- 3 tbsps coconut oil, melted
- 1 1/3 c. alkaline water

Directions:

1. Set your oven to 300 °F.
2. Combine all the dry ingredients in a bowl.
3. Add water and oil to the mixture and mix well.
4. Let the dough stay for 2–3 minutes.
5. Spread the dough evenly on a cookie sheet lined with parchment paper.
6. Bake for 30 minutes.
7. Reduce the oven heat to low and bake for another 30 minutes.
8. Crack the bread into bite-size pieces.
9. Serve.

Nutrition:

- Calories 248
- Total Fat 15.7 g.
- Saturated Fat 2.7 g.
- Cholesterol 75 mg.
- Sodium 94 mg.
- Total Carbohydrates 0.4 g.
- Fiber 0 g.
- Sugar 0 g.
- Protein 24.9 g.

80.   Spicy Roasted Nuts

Preparation time: 10 minutes

Servings: 4

Cooking time: 15 minutes

Ingredients:

- 8 oz. pecans or almonds or walnuts
- 1 tsp. sea salt
- 1 tbsp. olive oil or coconut oil
- 1 tsp. ground cumin
- 1 tsp. paprika powder or chili powder

Directions:

1. Add all the ingredients to a skillet.
2. Roast the nuts until golden brown.
3. Serve and enjoy.

Nutrition:

- Calories 287
- Total Fat 29.5 g.
- Saturated Fat 3 g.
- Cholesterol 0 mg.

- Total Carbohydrates 5.9 g.
- Sugar 1.4 g.
- Fiber 4.3 g.
- Sodium 388 mg.
- Protein 4.2 g.

81.   Wheat Crackers

Preparation time: 10 minutes

Servings: 4

Cooking time: 20 minutes

Ingredients:

- 1 3/4 c. almond flour
- 1 1/2 c. coconut flour
- 3/4 tsp. sea salt
-

- 1/3 c. vegetable oil
- 1 c. alkaline water
- Sea salt for sprinkling

Directions:

1. Set your oven to 350 °F.
2. Mix the coconut flour, almond flour, and salt in a bowl.
3. Stir in vegetable oil and water. Mix well until smooth.
4. Spread this dough on a floured surface into a thin sheet.
5. Cut small squares out of this sheet.
6. Arrange the dough squares on a baking sheet lined with parchment paper.
7. For about 20 minutes, bake until light golden in color.
8. Serve.

Nutrition:

- Calories 64
- Total Fat 9.2 g.
- Saturated Fat 2.4 g.
- Cholesterol 110 mg

- Sodium 276 mg
- Total Carbohydrates 9.2 g.
- Fiber 0.9 g.
- Sugar 1.4 g.
- Protein 1.5 g.

82.   Veggie Fritters

Preparation time: 5 minutes

Servings: 2

Cooking time: 10 minutes

Ingredients:

- 1 bell pepper
- 2 onions

- 2 c. mushrooms
- 1 tsp of sea salt
- 1 tbsp. onion powder
- 1 tsp. oregano
- 1 tbsp. basil
- A pinch cayenne
- 1 c. chickpea flour
- 1 tbsp. grapeseed oil

Directions:

1. Clean and chop the vegetables into small chunks. Not too small. Transfer the vegetables into a bowl and add all the seasonings.
2. Stir everything and let sit for about 5 minutes. Stir in chickpea flour, then add 1/2 c of water.
3. Stir while adding more flour until the desired consistency. Make sure everything holds nicely.
4. Heat a pan, then add oil but not too much. Spoon the fritter mix into the pan, creating little mounds.
5. Now cook for about 2–3 minutes until brown underneath and crispy. Flip and slightly press down to flatter them. Cook for about 2 minutes. Serve and Enjoy.

Nutrition:

- Calories 522
- Protein 24 g.
- Fiber 22.5 g.
- Fat 11 g.
- Carbohydrates 82.1 g.

83. Zucchini Pepper Chips

Preparation time: 10 minutes

Servings: 4

Cooking time: 15 minutes

Ingredients:

- 1 2/3 c. vegetable oil
- 1 tsp. garlic powder
- 1 tsp. onion powder
- 1/2 tsp. black pepper
- 3 tbsps crushed red pepper flakes
- 2 zucchinis, thinly sliced

Directions:

1. Mix oil with all the spices in a bowl.
2. Add zucchini slices and mix well.
3. Transfer the mixture to a Ziploc bag and seal it.
4. Refrigerate for 10 minutes.
5. Spread the zucchini slices on a greased baking sheet.
6. Bake for 15 minutes
7. Serve.

Nutrition:

- Calories 172
- Total Fat 11.1 g.
- Saturated Fat 5.8 g.
- Cholesterol 610 mg.
- Sodium 749 mg.
- Total Carbohydrates 19.9 g.
- Fiber 0.2 g.
- Sugar 0.2 g.
- Protein 13.5 g.

84.   Apple Chips

Preparation time: 5 minutes

Servings: 4

Cooking time: 45 minutes

Ingredients:

- 2 Golden Delicious apples, cored and thinly sliced

- 1 1/2 tsps. white sugar
- 1/2 tsp. ground cinnamon

Directions:

1. Set your oven to 225 °F.
2. Place the apple slices on a baking sheet.
3. Sprinkle sugar and cinnamon over the apple slices.
4. Bake for 45 minutes.
5. Serve.

Nutrition:

- Calories 127
- Total Fat 3.5 g.
- Saturated Fat 0.5 g.
- Cholesterol 162 mg

- Sodium 142 mg
- Total Carbohydrates 33.6 g.
- Fiber 0.4 g.
- Sugar 0.5 g.
- Protein 4.5 g.

85.   Kale Crisps

Preparation time: 10 minutes

Servings: 4

Cooking time: 10 minutes

Ingredients:

- 1 bunch kale, remove the stems, leaves torn into even pieces

- 1 tbsp. olive oil
- 1 tsp. sea salt

Directions:

1. Set your oven to 350 °F. Layer a baking sheet with parchment paper.
2. Spread the kale leaves on a paper towel to absorb all the moisture.
3. Toss the leaves with sea salt, and olive oil.
4. Kindly spread them, on the baking sheet and bake for 10 minutes.
5. Serve.

Nutrition:

- Calories 113
- Total Fat 7.5 g.

- Saturated Fat 1.1 g.
- Cholesterol 20 mg
- Sodium 97 mg
- Total Carbohydrates 1.4 g.

- Fiber 0 g.
- Sugar 0 g.
- Protein 1.1 g.

86.   Carrot Chips

Preparation time: 5 minutes

Cooking time: 12 minutes

Servings: 4

Ingredients:

- 4 carrots, washed, peeled and sliced
- 2 tsps. extra-virgin olive oil
- 1/4 tsp. sea salt

Directions:

1. Set your oven to 350 °F.
2. Toss carrots with salt and olive oil.
3. Spread the slices into two baking sheets in a single layer.
4. Bake for 6 minutes on upper and lower rack of the oven.
5. Switch the baking racks and bake for another 6 minutes.
6. Serve.

Nutrition:

- Calories 153
- Total Fat 7.5 g.
- Saturated Fat 1.1 g.
- Cholesterol 20 mg.
- Sodium 97 mg.
- Total Carbohydrates 20.4 g.
- Fiber 0 g.
- Sugar 0 g.
- Protein 3.1 g.

Chapter 15. Dessert

87.   Peanut Butter c.

Preparation time: 5 minutes

Cooking time: 10 minutes

Servings: 4

Ingredients:

- 1 packet plain gelatin
- 1/4 c. sugar substitute
- 2 c. nonfat cream
- 1/2 teaspoon vanilla
- 1/4 c. low-fat peanut butter
- 2 tbsps unsalted peanuts, chopped

Directions:

1. Mix gelatin, sugar substitute, and cream in a pan.
2. Let sit for 5 minutes.
3. Place over medium heat and cook until gelatin has been dissolved.
4. Stir in vanilla and peanut butter.
5. Pour into custard cups. Chill for 3 hours.
6. Top with the peanuts and serve.

Nutrition:

- Calories 171
- Carbohydrate 21 g.
- Protein 6.8 g.

88.   Fruit Pizza

Preparation time: 5 minutes

Cooking time: 10 minutes

Servings: 4

Ingredients:

- 1 tsp. maple syrup
- 1/4 tsp. vanilla extract
- 1/2 c. coconut milk yogurt
- 2 round slices watermelon
- 1/2 c. blackberries, sliced
- 1/2 c. strawberries, sliced
- 2 tbsps coconut flakes, unsweetened

Directions:

1. Mix maple syrup, vanilla, and yogurt in a bowl.
2. Spread the mixture on top of the watermelon slice.
3. Top with the berries and coconut flakes.

Nutrition:

- Calories 70
- Carbohydrate 14.6 g.
- Protein 1.2 g.

89. Choco Peppermint Cake

Preparation time: 5 minutes   **Servings:** 4

Cooking time: 10 minutes

Ingredients:

- Cooking spray
- 1/3 c. oil
- 15 oz. package chocolate cake mix

- 3 eggs, beaten
- 1 c. water
- 1/4 tsp. peppermint extract

Directions:

1. Spray a slow cooker with oil.
2. Mix all the ingredients in a bowl.
3. Use an electric mixer on medium speed setting to mix ingredients for 2 minutes.
4. Pour mixture into the slow cooker.
5. Cover the pot and cook on low for 3 hours.
6. Let cool before slicing and serving.

Nutrition:

- Calories 185
- Carbohydrate 27 g.
- Protein 3.8 g.

90. Roasted Mango

Preparation time: 5 minutes   **Servings:** 4

Cooking time: 10 minutes

Ingredients:

- 2 mangoes, sliced
- 2 tsps. crystallized ginger, chopped

- 2 tsps. orange zest
- 2 tbsps coconut flakes, unsweetened

Directions:

1. Preheat your oven to 350 °F.
2. Add mango slices in custard cups.
3. Top with the ginger, orange zest, and coconut flakes.
4. Bake in the oven for 10 minutes.

Nutrition:

- Calories 89

- Carbohydrate 20 g.
- Protein 0.8 g.

91.   Roasted Plums

Preparation time: 5 minutes

Servings: 4

Cooking time: 10 minutes

Ingredients:

- Cooking spray
- 6 plums, sliced
- 1/2 c. pineapple juice, unsweetened

- 1 tbsp. brown sugar
- 1/4 tsp. ground cardamom
- 1/2 teaspoon ground cinnamon
- 1/8 tsp. ground cumin

Directions:

1. Combine all the ingredients in a baking pan.
2. Roast in the oven at 450 °F for 20 minutes.

Nutrition:

- Calories 102

- Carbohydrate 18.7 g.
- Protein 2 g.

92.   Figs with Honey and Yogurt

Preparation time: 5 minutes

Servings: 4

Cooking time: 10 minutes

Ingredients:

- 1/2 teaspoon vanilla
- 8 oz. nonfat yogurt

- 2 figs, sliced
- 1 tbsp. walnuts, chopped and toasted
- 2 tsps. honey

Directions:

1. Stir vanilla into yogurt.
2. Mix well.
3. Top with the figs and sprinkle with walnuts.
4. Drizzle with honey and serve.

Nutrition:

- Calories 157
- Carbohydrate 24 g.
- Protein 7 g.

93. Lava Cake

Preparation time: 10 minutes

Cooking time: 10 minutes

Servings: 2

Ingredients:

- 2 oz of dark chocolate; you should at least use chocolate of 85 % cocoa solids
- 1 tbsp of super-fine almond flour
- 2 oz of unsalted almond butter
- 2 big eggs
- Pomegranate seeds

Directions:

1. Heat your oven to a temperature of about 350 °F.
2. Grease 2 heat proof ramekins with almond butter.
3. Now, melt the chocolate and the almond butter and stir very well.
4. Beat the eggs very well with a mixer.
5. Add the eggs to the chocolate and the butter mixture and mix very well with almond flour; then stir.
6. Pour the dough into 2 ramekins.
7. Bake for about 9–10 minutes.
8. Turn the cakes over plates and serve with pomegranate seeds!

Nutrition:

- Calories 459
- Carbohydrates 3 5 g.
- Fiber 0.8 g.

94. Cheese Cake

Preparation time: 15 minutes

Cooking time: 50 minutes

Servings: 6

Ingredients:

For the Almond Flour Cheesecake Crust

- 2 c of blanched almond flour
- 1/3 c of almond butter
- 3 tbsps of erythritol (powdered or granular)
- 1 tsp of vanilla extract

For the Keto Cheesecake Filling

- 32 oz of softened cream cheese
- 1 1/4 c of powdered erythritol
- 3 large eggs
- 1 tbsp of lemon juice
- 1 tsp of vanilla extract

Directions:

1. Preheat your oven to a temperature of about 350 °F.
2. Grease a spring form pan of 9 in. with cooking spray or just line its bottom with a parchment paper.

3. In order to make the cheesecake rust, stir in the melted butter, the almond flour, the vanilla extract, and the erythritol in a large bowl.
4. The dough will be a bit crumbly; so, press it into the bottom of your prepared tray.
5. Bake for about 12 minutes; then let cool for about 10 minutes.
6. In the meantime, beat the softened cream cheese and the powdered sweetener at a low speed until it becomes smooth.
7. Crack in the eggs and beat them in at a low to medium speed until it becomes fluffy. Make sure to add one a time.
8. Add in the lemon juice and the vanilla extract and mix at a low to medium speed with a mixer.
9. Pour your filling into your pan right on top of the crust. You can use a spatula to smooth the top of the cake.
10. Bake for about 45–50 minutes.
11. Remove the baked cheesecake from your oven and run a knife around its edge.
12. Let the cake cool for about 4 hours in the refrigerator.
13. Serve and enjoy your delicious cheese cake!

Nutrition:

- Calories 325
- Carbohydrates 6 g.
- Fiber 1 g.

95. Madeleine

Preparation time: 10 minutes

Servings: 12

Cooking time: 15 minutes

Ingredients:

- 2 large pastured eggs
- 3/4 c of almond flour
- 1 1/2 tbsps of swerve
- 1/4 c of cooled, melted coconut oil
- 1 tsp of vanilla extract
- 1 tsp of almond extract
- 1 tsp of lemon zest
- 1/4 tsp of salt

Directions:

1. Preheat your oven to a temperature of about 350 °F.
2. Combine the eggs with the salt and whisk on a high speed for about 5 minutes.
3. Slowly add in the swerve and keep mixing on high for 2 additional minutes.
4. Stir in the almond flour until it is very well-incorporated; then add in the vanilla and the almond extracts.
5. Add in the melted coconut oil and stir all your ingredients together.
6. Pour the obtained batter into equal parts in a greased madeleine tray.
7. Bake your Ketogenic Madeleine for about 13 minutes or until the edges start to have a brown color.
8. Flip the madeleines out of the baking tray.

Nutrition:

- Calories 87
- Carbohydrates 3 g.
- Fiber 3 g.

96.   Waffles

Preparation time: 20 minutes   **Servings:** 3

Cooking time: 30 minutes

Ingredients:

For the Ketogenic Waffles

- 8 oz of cream cheese
- 5 large pastured eggs
- 1/3 c of coconut flour
- 1/2 tsp of xanthan gum
- 1 pinch of salt
- 1/2 tsp of vanilla extract
- 2 tbsps of swerve
- 1/4 tsp of baking soda
- 1/3 c of almond milk

- 1/2 tsp of cinnamon pie spice
- 1/4 tsp of almond extract

For the Low-Carb Maple Syrup

- 1 c of water
- 1 tbsp of maple flavor
- 3/4 c of powdered swerve
- 1 tbsp of almond butter
- 1/2 tsp of xanthan gum

Optional Ingredients:

-

Directions:

1. To make the waffles: Make sure all your ingredients are exactly at room temperature.
2. Place all your ingredients for the waffles from cream cheese to pastured eggs, coconut flour, Xanthan gum, salt, vanilla extract, the Swerve, and the baking soda, except for the almond milk, with the help of a processor.
3. Blend your ingredients until it becomes smooth and creamy; then transfer the batter to a bowl.
4. Add the almond milk and mix your ingredients with a spatula.
5. Heat a waffle maker to a temperature of high.
6. Spray your waffle maker with coconut oil and add about 1/4 of the batter in it evenly with a spatula into your waffle iron.
7. Close your waffle and cook until you get the color you want.
8. Carefully remove the waffles to a platter.
9. For the ketogenic maple syrup: Place 1 1/4 c of water, the swerve, and the maple in a small pan and bring to a boil over a low heat; then let simmer for about 10 minutes.
10. Add the almond butter.
11. Sprinkle the Xanthan gum over the top of the waffle and use an immersion blender to blend smoothly.
12. Serve and enjoy your delicious waffles!

Nutrition:

- Calories 316
- Carbohydrates 7 g.
- Fiber 3 g.

97.   Pretzels

Preparation time: 10 minutes

Servings: 8

Cooking time: 20 minutes

Ingredients:

- 1 1/2 c of pre-shredded mozzarella
- 2 tbsps of full fat cream cheese
- 1 large egg
- 3/4 c of almond flour+ 2 tbsps of ground almonds or almond meal
- 1/2 tsp of baking powder
- 1 pinch of coarse sea salt

Directions:

1. Heat your oven to a temperature of about 180 °C/356 °F.
2. Melt the cream cheese and the mozzarella cheese and stir over a low heat until the cheeses are perfectly melted.
3. If you choose to microwave the cheese, just do that for about 1 minute, no more; and if you want to do it on the stove, turn off the heat as soon as the cheese is completely melted.
4. Add the large egg to the prepared warm dough; then stir until your ingredients are very well combined. If the egg is cold; you will need to heat it gently.
5. Add in the ground almonds or the almond flour and the baking powder and stir until your ingredients are very well combined.
6. Take one pinch of the dough of cheese and toll it or stretch it in your hands until it is about 18–20 cm of length; if your dough is sticky, you can oil your hands to avoid that.
7. Now, form pretzels from the cheese dough and nicely shape it; then place it over a baking sheet.
8. Sprinkle with a little bit of salt and bake for about 17 minutes.

Nutrition:

- Calories 113
- Carbohydrates 2.5 g.
- Fiber 0.8 g.

98.   Cheesy Taco Bites

Preparation time: 5 minutes

Servings: 12

Cooking time: 10 minutes

Ingredients:

- 2 c of packaged shredded cheddar cheese
- 2 tbsp of chili powder
- 2 tbsps of cumin
- 1 tsp of salt
- 8 tsps of coconut cream for garnishing
- Use Pico de Gallo for garnishing as well

Directions:

1. Preheat your oven to a temperature of about 350 °F.
2. Over a baking sheet lined with a parchment paper, place 1 tbsp. piles of cheese and make sure to a space of 2 in. between each.
3. Place the baking sheet in your oven and bake for about 5 minutes.

4. Remove from the oven and let the cheese cool down for about 1 minute; then carefully lift up and press each into the cups of a mini muffin tin.
5. Make sure to press the edges of the cheese to form the shape of mini muffins.
6. Let the cheese cool completely; then remove it.
7. Fill the cheese cups with the coconut cream, then top with Pico de Gallo.

Nutrition:

- Calories 73

- Carbohydrates 3 g.
- Protein 4 g.

99. Nut Squares

Preparation time: 30 minutes

Cooking time: 10 minutes

Servings: 10

Ingredients:

- 2 c of almonds, pumpkin seeds, sunflower seeds, and walnuts
- 1/2 c of desiccated coconut
- 1 tbsp of chia seeds
- 1/4 tsp of salt
- 2 tbsps of coconut oil
- 1 tsp of vanilla extract
- 3 tbsps of almond or peanut butter
- 1/3 c of Sukrin Gold Fiber Syrup

Directions:

1. Line a square baking tin with a baking paper; then lightly grease it with cooking spray.
2. Chop all the nuts roughly; then slightly grease it; you can also leave them as whole.
3. Mix the nuts in a large bowl; then combine them with the coconut, the chia seeds, and the salt.
4. In a microwave-proof bowl; add the coconut oil; then add the vanilla, the almond butter, and the fiber syrup and microwave the mixture for about 30 seconds.
5. Stir your ingredients together very well; then pour the melted mixture right on top of the nuts.
6. Press the mixture into your prepared baking tin with the help of the back of a measuring cup and push very well.
7. Freeze your treat for about 1 hour before cutting it.
8. Cut your frozen nut batter into small cubes or squares of the same size.

Nutrition:

- Calories 268
- Carbohydrates 14 g.
- Fiber 1 g.

Chapter 16. Smoothies and Juice

100. Dandelion Avocado Smoothie

Preparation time: 15 minutes

Servings: 1

Cooking time: 0

Ingredients:

- 1 c of dandelion
- 1 orange, juiced

- Coconut water
- 1 avocado
- 1 key lime, juiced

Directions:

1. In a high-speed blender until smooth, blend the ingredients.

Nutrition:

- Calories 160
- Fat 15 g.

- Carbohydrates 9 g.
- Protein 2 g.

101. Amaranth Greens and Avocado Smoothie

Preparation time: 15 minutes

Cooking time: 0

Servings: 1

Ingredients:

- 1 key lime, juice
- 2 sliced apples, seeded
- 1/2 avocado

- 2 cupsful of amaranth greens
- 2 cupsful of watercress
- 1 cupful of water

Directions:

1. Add the whole recipes together and transfer them into the blender. Blend thoroughly until smooth.

Nutrition:

- Calories 160
- Fat 15 g.
- Carbohydrates 9 g.
- Protein 2 g.

102. Lettuce, Orange, and Banana Smoothie

Preparation time: 15 minutes

Servings: 1

Cooking time: 0

Ingredients:

- 1 and a half cupsful of fresh lettuce
- 1 large banana

- 1 cup of mixed berries of your choice
- 1 juiced orange

Directions:

1. First, add the orange juice to your blender.
2. Add the remaining ingredients and blend thoroughly.
3. Enjoy!

Nutrition:

- Calories 252.1
- Protein 4.1 g.

103. Delicious Elderberry Smoothie

Preparation time: 15 minutes

Cooking time: 0

Servings: 1

Ingredients:

- 1 cupful of Elderberry
- 1 cupful of Cucumber
- 1 large apple
- 1/4 cupful of water

Directions:

1. Add the whole ingredients together into a blender. Grind very well until they are uniformly smooth and enjoy.

Nutrition:

- Calories 106
- Carbohydrates 26.68 g.

104. Peaches Zucchini Smoothie

Preparation time: 15 minutes   **Servings:** 1

Cooking time: 0

Ingredients:

- 1/4 cupful of coconut water
- 1/2 cupful of zucchini

- 1/2 cupful of squash.
- 1/2 cupful of peaches

Directions:

1. Add the whole ingredients together into a blender and blend until smooth and serve.

Nutrition:

- Sodium 10 mg.
- Carbohydrate 14 g.
- Fiber 2 g.

- Calories 55
- Fat 0 g.
- Protein 2 g.

105. Ginger Orange and Strawberry Smoothie

Preparation time: 15 minutes   **Servings:** 1

Cooking time: 0

Ingredients:

- 1 c of strawberry
- 1 large orange, juice
- 1 large banana
- 1/4 small sized ginger, peeled and sliced
- Water

Directions:

2. Transfer the orange juice to a clean blender.
3. Add the remaining ingredients and blend thoroughly until smooth.
4. Enjoy!

Nutrition:

- Calories 32
- Fat 0.3 g.
- Protein 2 g.
- Sodium 10 mg.
- Carbohydrate 14 g.
- Fiber 2 g.

106. Kale Parsley and Chia Seeds Detox Smoothie

Preparation time: 15 minutes

Servings: 1

Cooking time: 0

Ingredients:

- 3 tbsp. chia seeds, grounded
- 1 cupful of water
- 1 sliced banana
- 1 pear, chopped

- 1 cupful of organic kale
- 1 cupful of parsley
- Two tbsp of lemon juice.
- A dash of cinnamon.

Directions:

1. Add the whole ingredients together into a blender and pour the water before blending. Blend at high speed until smooth and enjoy. You may or may not place it in the refrigerator depending on how hot or cold the weather appears.

Nutrition:

- Calories 75
- Fat 1 g.

- Protein 5 g.
- Fiber 10 g.

107. Watermelon Lemonade

Preparation time: 5 minutes

Cooking time: 0 minutes

Servings: 6

Ingredients:

- 4 c. diced watermelon
- 4 c. cold water

- 2 tbsps freshly squeezed lemon juice
- 1 tbsp. freshly squeezed lime juice

Directions:

1. In a blender, combine the watermelon, water, lemon juice, and lime juice, and blend for 1 minute.
2. Strain the contents through a fine-mesh sieve or nut-milk bag. Serve chilled. Store in the refrigerator for up to 3 days.

Serving tip: Slice up a few lemon or lime wedges to serve with your Watermelon Lemonade, or top it with a few fresh mint leaves to give it an extra-crisp, minty flavor.

Nutrition:

- Calories 60

108. Bubbly Orange Soda

Preparation time: 5 minutes   **Servings:** 4

Cooking time: 0 minutes

Ingredients:

- 4 c. carbonated water
- 2 c. pulp-free orange juice (4 oranges, freshly squeezed and strained)

Directions:

1. For each serving, pour 2 parts carbonated water and 1-part orange juice over ice right before serving.
2. Stir and enjoy.

Serving tip: This recipe is best made right before drinking. The amount of fizz in the carbonated water will decrease the longer it's open, so if you're going to make it ahead of time, make sure it's stored in an airtight, refrigerator-safe container.

Nutrition:

- Calories 56

109. Creamy Cashew Milk

Preparation time: 5 minutes   **Servings:** 8

Cooking time: 0 minutes

Ingredients:

- 1/4 c. raw cashews, soaked overnight
- 4 c. water

Directions:

1. In a blender, blend the water and cashews on high speed for 2 minutes.
2. Strain with a nut-milk bag or cheesecloth, then store in the refrigerator for up to 5 days.

Variation tip: This recipe makes unsweetened cashew milk that can be used in savory and sweet dishes. For a creamier version to put in your coffee, cut the amount of water in half. For a sweeter version, add 1–2 tbsps maple syrup and 1 tsp. vanilla extract before blending.

Nutrition:

- Calories 18

110. Homemade Oat Milk

Preparation time: 5 minutes

Servings: 8

Cooking time: 0 minutes

Ingredients:

- 4 c. water

- 1 c. rolled oats

Directions:

1. Put the oats in a medium bowl, and cover with cold water. Soak for 15 minutes, then drain and rinse the oats.
2. Pour the cold water and the soaked oats into a blender. Blend for 60–90 seconds, or just until the mixture is a creamy white color throughout. (Blending any further may over blend the oats, resulting in a gummy milk.)
3. Strain through a nut-milk bag or colander, then store in the refrigerator for up to 5 days.

Variation tip: This recipe can easily be made into chocolate oat milk. Once you've strained the oat milk, return it to a blender with 3 tbsps cocoa powder, 2 tbsps maple syrup, and 1 tsp. vanilla extract, then blend for 30 seconds.

Nutrition:

- Calories 39

111. **Lucky Mint Smoothie**

Preparation time: 5 minutes

Servings: 2

Cooking time: 0 minutes

Ingredients:

- 1 tbsp. fresh mint leaves or 1/4 tsp. peppermint extract
- 2 c. plant-based milk
- 1 tsp. vanilla extract
- 2 frozen bananas, halved

Directions:

1. In a blender, combine the milk, bananas, mint, and vanilla. Blend on high for 1–2 minutes, or until the contents reach a smooth and creamy consistency, and serve.

Variation tip: If you like to sneak greens into smoothies, add a cup or two of spinach to boost the health benefits of this smoothie and give it an even greener appearance.

Nutrition:

- Calories 152

112.   Paradise Island Smoothie

Preparation time: 5 minutes

Cooking time: 0 minutes

Servings: 2

Ingredients:

- 2 c. plant-based milk
- 1 frozen banana
- 1/2 c. frozen mango chunks
- 1/2 c. frozen pineapple chunks
- 1 tsp. vanilla extract

Directions:

1. In a blender, combine the milk, banana, mango, pineapple, and vanilla. Blend on high for 1–2 minutes, or until the contents reach a smooth and creamy consistency, and serve.

Leftover tip: If you have any leftover smoothie, you can put it in a jar with some rolled oats and allow the mixture to soak in the refrigerator overnight to create a tropical version of overnight oats.

Nutrition:

- Calories 176

Conclusion

Diabetes is a serious condition caused by a deficiency of insulin. Insulin is a hormone that is necessary for the proper functioning of the body. When a person develops diabetes, the cells in the body do not respond to insulin properly. The result is that the cells do not get the energy and nutrients they need, and then they start to die.

Being diagnosed with diabetes will bring some major changes in your lifestyle. From the time you are diagnosed with it, it would always be a constant battle with the food. You need to become a lot more careful with your food choices and the quantity that you ate. Every meal will feel like a major effort. You will be planning every day for the whole week, well in advance. Depending upon the type of food you ate, you have to keep checking your blood sugar levels. You may get used to taking long breaks between meals and staying away from snacks between dinner and breakfast.

Food would be treated as a bomb like it can go off at any time. According to an old saying, "When the body gets too hot, then your body heads straight to the kitchen."

Managing diabetes can be a very, very stressful ordeal. There will be many times that you will mark your glucose levels down on a piece of paper like you are plotting graph lines or something. You will mix your insulin shots up and then stress about whether or not you are giving yourself the right dosage. You will always be over-cautious because it involves a lot of math and a really fine margin of error. But now, those days are gone!

With the help of technology and books, you can stock your kitchen with the right foods, like meal plans, diabetic friendly dishes, etc. You can also get an app that will even do the work for you. You can also people-watch on the internet and find the know-how to cook and eat right; you will always be a few meals away from certain disasters, like a plummeting blood sugar level. Always carry some sugar in your pocket. You won't have to experience the pangs of hunger but if you are unlucky, you will have to ration your food and bring along some simple low-calorie snacks with you.

This is the future of diabetes.

As you've reached the end of this book, you have gained complete control of your diabetes and this is just the beginning of your journey towards a better, healthier life. I hope I was able to inculcate some knowledge into you and make this adventure a little bit less of a struggle.

I would like to remind you that you're not alone in having to manage this disease and that nearly 85 % of the new cases are 20 years old or younger.

Regardless of the length or seriousness of your diabetes, it can be managed! Take the information presented here and start with it!

Preparation is key to having a healthier and happier life.

It's helpful to remember that every tool at your disposal can help in some way.

Index

K

Kale and White Bean Stew; 32

Kale Chips; 72

Kale Crisps; 102

Kale Parsley and Chia Seeds Detox Smoothie; 123

Kale Pesto's Pasta; 58

L

Lamb with Broccoli and Carrots; 88

Lava Cake; 110

Lettuce, Orange, and Banana Smoothie; 119

Lighter Eggplant Parmesan; 34

Lighter Shrimp Scampi; 37

Lime-Parsley Lamb Cutlets; 53

Lovely Porridge; 29

Lucky Mint Smoothie; 128

M

Madeleine; 112

Maple-Mustard Salmon; 38

Mediterranean Lamb Meatballs; 90

Mediterranean Steak Sandwiches; 54

Millet Pilaf; 41

Mushroom, Zucchini, and Onion Frittata; 26

N

Nut Squares; 116

O

Orange-Marinated Pork Tenderloin; 51

P

Paradise Island Smoothie; 129

Parsnip, Carrot, and Kale Salad with Dressing; 64

Peach Muesli Bake; 23

Peaches Zucchini Smoothie; 121

Peanut Butter c.; 104

Pork Chop Diane; 48

Pork Chops with Grape Sauce; 79

Pork with Cranberry Relish; 81

Pretzels; 114

Pumpkin Spice Crackers; 96

R

Roasted Asparagus and Red Peppers; 76

Roasted Delicata Squash with Thyme; 75

Roasted Mango; 107

Roasted Plums; 108

Roasted Pork and Apples; 80

Roasted Vegetables; 40

Rosemary Lamb; 89

S

Sautéed Collard Greens and Cabbage; 74

Sesame Pork with Mustard Sauce; 82

Simple Deviled Eggs; 73

Slow Cooker Two-Bean Sloppy Joes; 33

Spicy Jalapeno Popper Deviled Eggs; 28

Spicy Roasted Nuts; 97

Spinach and Cheese Quiche; 27

Spinach and Orange Salad with Oil Drizzle; 61

Steak with Mushroom Sauce; 83

Steak with Tomato and Herbs; 84

Steel-Cut Oatmeal Bowl with Fruit and Nuts; 24

Stuffed Mushrooms; 46

Stuffed Portobello with Cheese; 36

T

Tarragon Spring Peas; 77

Thai Quinoa Salad; 55

Tomato Toasts; 65

Printed in Great Britain
by Amazon